EDUCATION OF THE INFANT AND YOUNG CHILD

Contributors

JEROME S. BRUNER
VICTOR H. DENENBERG
JEROME KAGAN
DOLORES Z. LAMBIE
WILLIAM A. MASON
RICHARD E. ORTON
HANŬS PAPOUŠEK
EARL S. SCHAEFER
DAVID P. WEIKART

Education of the Infant and Young Child

Edited By

Victor H. Denenberg

*Departments of Biobehavioral
Sciences and Psychology
University of Connecticut
Storrs, Connecticut*

1970

New York and London

ACADEMIC PRESS, INC.
111 Fifth Avenue, New York, New York 10003

United Kingdom Edition published by
ACADEMIC PRESS, INC. (LONDON) LTD.
Berkeley Square House, London W1X 6BA

LIBRARY OF CONGRESS CATALOG CARD NUMBER: 77-137617

PRINTED IN THE UNITED STATES OF AMERICA

Contents

v

List of Contributors

Numbers in parentheses indicate the pages on which the authors'
contributions begin.

JEROME S. BRUNER (109), Department of Psychology, Harvard University, Cambridge, Massachusetts

VICTOR H. DENENBERG (1, 125), Departments of Biobehavioral Sciences and Psychology, University of Connecticut, Storrs, Connecticut

JEROME KAGAN (5), Department of Social Relations, Harvard University, Cambridge, Massachusetts

DOLORES Z. LAMBIE (83), High/Scope Educational Research Foundation, Ypsilanti, Michigan

WILLIAM A. MASON (25), Behavioral Sciences, Delta Regional Primate Research Center, Covington, Louisiana

RICHARD E. ORTON (117), Office of Child Development, Department of Health, Education and Welfare, Washington, D. C.

HANUŠ PAPOUŠEK (51), Institute for the Care of Mother and Child, Prague, Czechoslovakia

EARL S. SCHAEFER (61), Center for Studies of Child and Family Mental Health, National Institute of Mental Health, Chevy Chase, Maryland

DAVID P. WEIKART (83), High/Scope Educational Research Foundation, Ypsilanti, Michigan

Preface

It has been apparent for some time that there is a trend toward earlier formal educational experiences with children to the point where infants are now involved in certain experimental programs. Because the potential for influencing and controlling behavior becomes greater as one works with younger children, this shift toward earlier educational experiences raises some serious questions concerning their long-term consequences. Of immediate concern are the many infants and young children who are now or who will shortly be involved in formal or informal educational programs in day-care centers. The number of such centers in this country has increased considerably in the past few years, and it is apparent that the trend is going to continue. Indeed, there is a good likelihood that the federal government will supply much of the money needed to build and to run day-care centers.

The purpose of this book is to bring together information which is relevant to our understanding of the effects of early educational experiences, including those experiences which are unique to day-care centers. This information comes from a wide variety of sources, including experimental studies with animals, research on the effects of socioeconomic class membership, investigations of the effects of different types of preschool curricula, studies on the effects of early educational environments, and observations on specific characteristics of day-care centers in a number of European countries. The reader will find in the various papers both specific practical suggestions concerning what should and should not be done in a day-care center, as well as a variety of research ideas and theoretical positions. Thus, the book will be of value to the applied person, the researcher, and the theoretician who are concerned with the general nature of early developmental processes and the particular question of the kinds of experiences to which the young infant should be exposed.

In a sense this book originated at a meeting of the Committee on Brain Sciences of the National Research Council of which I am a member. In one of our discussions I described my concern about the trend toward earlier educational experiences because of the large amount of research data from both animals and humans showing that experiences in very early life can have long-term and widespread effects upon a variety of behavioral and physiological characteristics. The committee members also thought this was an important issue, and, after some discussion, Neal Miller, Chairman of the Committee, suggested that I organize a symposium on this topic for the national meeting of the American Association for the Advancement of Science which was to take place in Boston in December, 1969. The Committee passed a motion to that effect, and I set up the symposium which was formally sponsored by the Section on Psychology of the AAAS in association with the National Research Council Committee on Brain Sciences.

We had an overflow audience of approximately 225 interested, enthusiastic, and knowledgeable people, with an age range from approximately 17 to 70. The speakers gave abbreviated versions of their papers so that there would be ample time for questions and discussion from the floor. The audience eagerly entered into discussion and debate with the speakers as well as with each other. The enthusiastic response of the audience was quite gratifying to all of the participants. I am just sorry that it is not possible to present in this book the many comments offered by members of the audience. There are audiotapes available of the meeting which may be purchased through the AAAS offices at 1515 Massachusetts Avenue NW, Washington, D. C. for those who are interested.

The papers in this book are expanded and more detailed versions of the papers which were presented at the AAAS meeting.

There are many people who helped make the symposium a success. Two of these people merit special citation: Dr. Louise Marshall, Executive Secretary for the Committee on Brain Sciences, who was extraordinarily helpful in many of the arrangements concerning the meeting, and Dr. Jerome Kagan, who made a number of valuable suggestions concerning the organization of the symposium and added his enthusiastic support to this venture.

Chapter 1

Introduction | *Victor H. Denenberg*

The reason I am involved in infant education is that I do experiments with animals on the effects of infantile stimulation and early experiences. And all of us who have been involved in such work—whether we manipulate experiences prenatally, during infancy, or during early postweaning development—have been profoundly impressed with the major changes of essentially a permanent nature which we bring about as a function of our experimental intervention. We are now at the point in our research where we can take an animal and, within broad limits, we can specify the "personality" of that animal as well as some of its behavioral capabilities by the appropriate manipulation of experiences in early life. For example, one can take a newborn rat and raise it under certain conditions so that in adulthood it will be highly emotional, relatively inefficient in learning, and less capable of withstanding environmental stresses and thus more likely to die from such stresses. On the other hand, we can also produce rats, through the appropriate experiences in early life, which are nonemotional, highly curious and investigatory, efficient learners, and which are less prone to physiological upset when exposed to mildly stressful situations. Other research has shown that we can create animals which are more intelligent in the sense of being better able to solve problems to get to a goal. Turning to a different realm of behavior, one can restrict the early experiences of rhesus monkeys so that, when adults, they act in a bizarre psychotic-like manner, show almost a complete absence of appropriate sexual behavior (this is true both for the male and for the female), and, in those few instances where the females have become pregnant, they exhibit a profound lack of appropriate maternal behavior.

1

Thus, the animal research on early experiences has shown that both "good" and "bad" effects can result from various regimens of experiences introduced at the appropriate times during development. And the research has also shown that these experiences will last for essentially the complete lifetime of the animal. Indeed, there have been some studies done with the rat which show that the offspring and the grandoffspring of females who have received certain forms of stimulation in infancy and early life have been affected by their mothers' and grandmothers' experiences. These effects are brought about through changes in the mother's and grandmother's behavior and physiology which act upon their offspring both during the prenatal period as well as during the weaning period.

The work which I have just cited—and this is only a minuscule amount of the experimental literature today—has been carried out with mammals. Since the human being is also a biological organism and a member of the class *Mammalia,* and since there is some degree of continuity between one phyletic level and another, it seems reasonable that the *general principle* derived from the animal work will also hold at the human level. This principle is: Stimulation and experiences during early development can have profound and permanent effects upon the behavioral and physiological capabilities of the organism. Thus, the "pure" basic animal research now has important practical implications by pointing to the neonatal and early infancy periods in the child's development as ones that are especially critical with respect to the child's future behavioral and physiological capabilities.

This problem can be brought into sharper focus by examining some of the social and educational consequences of proposed political legislation in the area of "early education." One of the trends is to shift the start of formal education to even earlier ages. At the present time there are a number of programs, including day-care centers, where very young children are exposed to a variety of educational experiences. If one projects this trend, it is highly likely that there will soon be day-care centers around the country which will be aimed at the very young child (6 months old) and particularly that segment of the population which is often called "culturally deprived." Indeed, a number of statements have been made by various federal officials to the effect that day-care centers will be established as a means of taking care of infants and young children.

One question of great concern is: What experiences should these infants receive in the day-care centers? We have seen that events occurring in very early life have long-lasting and powerful impacts upon developing organisms. Thus, the manipulation of experiences (educational, emotional, social, and others) in a day-care center offers the potential for great good or great harm.

The infant is our most important natural resource in the world today. His capability for assimilating and processing information in very early life as well as his capabilities for emotional reactivity and physiological involvement have been clearly documented. The growth and development of the infant into his adult capabilities are too important to be ignored on the national level and must be the subject of experimental investigation and effective evaluation.

As one small step toward this goal the purpose of this volume is to review and summarize data which are available at both the human and subhuman level concerning the effects of early experiences. Kagan will present some theoretical ideas as to why poor children do badly in school situations and he will suggest possible ways of preventing these deficits. Next there will be discussion and review of some of the animal research by Mason with special attention to the effects of early deprivation. After this, Papoušek will discuss his experiences with day-care centers in Czechoslovakia and his knowledge concerning other infant rearing centers in Eastern and Western Europe. The next chapter will be a review by Schaefer of his own research and that of others which clearly indicates the need for education (as broadly defined) to start very early in the infant's life experiences. The final contribution is by Weikart and Lambie who have been able to obtain marked changes in performance of very young children by several experimental regimens.

Following this set of papers are the comments of two

discussants who are uniquely qualified to talk on this topic. The
first discussant is Bruner whose work in cognitive studies both
with older children and infants is well known. The second
discussant is Orton, the Associate Director of Project Head Start,
who comments on the preceding chapters from the position of a
sympathetic Washington administrator responsible for managing
the largest and most important source of funds available in the
field of preschool education. Finally, the closing chapter is
presented to return us full circle to the problem of what we
should do with and for infants who are placed into day-care
centers.

Chapter 2

On Class Differences and Early Development | *Jerome Kagan*

One of the most serious problems facing this nation is the fact that children of poor families generally do not perform as well in school as children from more privileged families. Previous generations were not very distressed by this fact since school attendance and academic progress were not regarded, until recently, as necessary for economic survival in the society. The primary function of the school in earlier generations was character education and the preparation of a priest class, in both the literal and figurative sense of the word. Education, during the last 300 years, has been largely a ritual to preserve distinction among social classes and to lend some mystique to those who successfully withstood its rigors. Although the American view of public school has always been more practical than that of the European, Americans never seriously questioned the premise that school success was not absolutely necessary for adaptation to the community. A formal education was only required if the person wished to assume a role of power or leadership in the society. This plan has worked well. A person who persists for 16-20 years in the educational system with acceptable levels of performance and no sins on his record is a bit more likely to possess a sense of responsibility, perspective on human affairs, ability to delay gratification, and a capacity for leadership than one who never began the arduous journey or one who withdrew before it was over. Since the system worked efficiently, society was not overly concerned with school failures. Early failures indicated how sensitive the system was in eliminating those who were not of the proper temperament or ability to care or take responsibility for their fellow man.

We live today in a different time, the first time in the history of man that a minimum of 12 years of formal education has become necessary for economic survival. Hence, many citizens have become justifiably concerned with the school failures that were ignored in the past. We now realize that these failures are the basis of serious psychological disruption in the entire community, for the rate of failure among children from poor families is too high.

THE POOR CHILD AND SCHOOL FAILURE

The poor child's slower progress in mastery of school tasks is probably a function of many factors, the most salient of which are weaker motivation and expectancy of failure which lead, in turn, to fragmented attention and a reluctance to persist with difficult problems.

It should be made clear in the beginning of this chapter that learning to read, add, and write compositions are not to be regarded as the most sanctified set of childhood competences. They just happen to be among the dominant values of Western culture, values which are not likely to change in the immediate future. Since a society cannot afford to have a large segment of its population deficient in, or resistant to, acquiring the skills valued by the majority, it is necessary that either the value system of the society be changed, or the poor child learn these values and skills. The dominant belief among most parents and educators is that the latter alternative is more desirable. Although we often talk of lower vs. middle class children, a psychological, rather than an economic, definition of class is intended. The economic and sociological definition of class is based on three correlated characteristics—education, income, and vocation. From a psychological point of view, however, a critical attribute of class is a feeling of exploitation by another class, coupled with a sense of futility about effecting any change in one's life situation. The essential dimension of the concept "deprived" is the feeling of impotence to alter one's life or the future of one's children.

Although genetic factors may contribute to individual differences in a child's academic attainments, existing evidence is not inconsistent with the statement that the vast majority of school failures by children from deprived environments are primarily a function of experience. The validity of this conclusion rests on a dichotomy of competence into two basic classes: normative tasks, like walking, talking, reading, and writing, which all members of the species are capable of attaining; in contrast to exceptional talent at music, mathematics, or spatial reasoning. Genetic factors may play a role in influencing unusual degrees of competence, but are less likely to control differences in quality of functioning that are natural to the species. Dogs are bred for length of leg, and the range in this anatomical trait is enormous. As a result, some dogs attain running speeds that others can never attain. However, all dogs, from dachshund to greyhound, *can run.* That ability is natural to the species. Analogously, it is argued that the ability to understand language, to speak in coherent sentences, to manipulate numbers, to think symbolically, and to read are part of man's inheritance. The basic tasks posed by the American schools, therefore, are probably not beyond the capacity of any child with an intact nervous system.

REDUCING SCHOOL FAILURE IN POOR CHILDREN

If we accept this assumption, there are two alternative action programs that might be implemented to reduce the high proportion of poor children with academic difficulties. The first—that we change the value system of the society—we have already rejected. We could change the criteria of adaptation in the wider society, or allow each group in the society to develop its own criteria. One can argue that mastery of reading or writing should not be necessary for leadership, power, or economic survival. Although this is a possible alternative, it is not likely to be adopted.

A second alternative is to make psychological changes in the ecology of the lower class child in order to increase the probability that he will be more successful in attaining normative skills. To effect this goal we can change the school, change the environment in the preschool years, or go even further, and change the caretaker's relationship to the infant. Of course, simultaneous changes in all three systems are possible.

Changing the School

Changing the nature of the school may not be the most efficient way to gain the desired goal. Important aspects of the child's motivation and cognitive skills are established before he enters the first grade. The differences in language and number competence between lower and middle class children are significant by the time the child is 4 years old, and are awesome by the time he is in the third grade. This is not to say that a complete overhaul of the academic system would not be beneficial. Reducing classroom size so that each teacher has 10 rather than 30 pupils should make a difference. Individual instruction would be increased and these conditions might allow the school to effect highly desirable changes. This alternative should certainly be pursued. However, the lack of funds for such a change in the educational system lends a note of caution to this plan.

Changing the Preschool Environment

Alternatively one could concentrate on the preschool years,

2½-5. Although the headstart program has had minimal documented success, it never was an adequate test of the potential power of intervention during these years. The President and the administration, as many know, are entertaining the notion of instituting nationwide day-care centers. If these are implemented in a creative way we might influence the child in a desirable fashion. However, it must be appreciated that we do not have adequate theory or knowledge to decide on the best set of tutorial procedures to be used in day-care centers for preschool youngsters. This issue should have the highest priority.

Changing the Caretaker-Infant Relationship

A final strategy, not exclusive of the first two, is to change the mother's relationship with her infant. The idea for this suggestion rests on the assumption that a child's experiences with his adult caretaker during the first 24 months of life are major determinants of the quality of his motivation, expectancy of success, and cognitive abilities during the school years. In a moment we shall consider data in support of this position.

SOME DIFFERENCES BETWEEN POOR
AND PRIVILEGED CHILDREN

Many poor parents with young infants do not have clear understanding of how the child develops and do not have sufficient confidence that they can mold the infant in a way to match their ideal for him. The mother may know what kind of a 10-year-old she wants, but she is not certain what she should do to have a serious effect on the growth of the infant. She may hold fatalistic attitudes toward the young child, assuming that the power to sculpt him lies within his genetic potential and chance experiences in the environment over which she has no control. Consequently she does not interact with him as often, as long, or as consistently as the middle class mother. If we could increase the mother's sense of control over her infant's growth and persuade her of the value of language, motivation, and expectancy of success, she might begin to believe that her efforts with the infant could facilitate fulfillment of her ideals. It is likely that success in this venture would have salutary changes on the child.

There are seven major kinds of differences between poor and privileged children that emerge during the opening years of life which preview differences seen a half-decade later.

Language

The first category of difference includes comprehension and expression of language. The poor child is less able to understand complex sentences and speaks in simpler and shorter phrases. This difference may be the partial result of less frequent language interchange between mother and young child. Poor mothers engage in shorter periods of face-to-face talking with their infants than middle class mothers and do not speak to their child with the variety, complexity, and specificity that is typical of middle class mothers. Although television may help the lower class child acquire new vocabulary items, it is not as effective as direct communication from an adult because the language flowing from the television set is not directly related to the child's desires nor tailored to his competence.

Exposure to the language of others is most helpful when it is distinctive and comprehensible. The quality of language is much more critical than its quantity. This principle is seen in clear form in infancy when mothers are engaging in vocal play with their infants. The sequence typically begins with the baby babbling a string of meaningless cooing sounds. The mother talks back to the baby, the child responds, and the vocal ballet proceeds with each reacting to the other. Careful observation of the mother-infant interaction reveals that middle class mothers are more likely to engage in these reciprocal, face-to-face talking sequences in which the mother is not providing any distracting stimulation.

The lower class mother often spends as much time talking in the vicinity of her infant, but she may be changing a diaper, or filling a bottle, and her speech is not salient to the child. It is probably not a coincidence that middle class children are more talkative during the second year of life and make language distinctions lower class children do not. It is believed that if the lower class mother were to increase the amount of face-to-face talking, the child's language development might be facilitated.

Mental Set

A second factor involves the child's mental set to activate cognitive structures to solve problems or to understand discrepant events. A child's distribution of attention to the environment is governed, in large measure, by the quality of his cognitive structures and his tendency to activate these structures when he encounters an unusual event. Attention to an event leads spontaneously to the development of a relevant schema, where a schema is the mind's representation of the salient elements of that experience. A schema should be regarded as an abstract quality, much like gravity or temperature, that is a property of the mind.

A schema allows the child to recognize an event. Children with a rich set of schemata for a class of events maintain attention to variations in the environment until they have explained them. Children differ in the tendency to activate existing schemata to explain discrepant events, as well as in the richness of these schemata. One of the possible reasons for these differences is that the middle class mother unconsciously plays "theme and variations" with her infant. For example, she plays peek-a-boo, and as the child becomes bored with a particular variation, she shifts the locus of her face or changes her facial expression in order to keep her child laughing and attentive. This simple practice repeated day after day, week after week, teaches the child that attention to unexpected derivatives of an unusual event may lead to renewed cognitive excitement. The child learns "to be prepared" for a moderate surprise. This mental preparation for the unusual is critical for new learning.

Attachment

A third difference between infants involves attachment to an adult. Infants of most vertebrate species are born with a set of behaviors that they normally direct to the biological mother because she is the living creature most often present. Infant monkeys grasp and cling to the hairy undersurface of the mother; infant ducks follow the mother immediately after hatching. Human infants can neither follow nor grasp the mother, but they can visually scan, suck, smile, babble, and cling, and later, play reciprocally with an adult. Normally the infant directs these responses toward the biological mother. Continued display of these reactions toward the mother leads the infant to become attached to her, much as adults become attached to a frequently used object or place—a favorite pipe, chair, or summer cabin.

Attachment to an object is the predisposition to make responses toward the object, and to search for that object when one feels distress, fear, or anxiety. The attached child becomes receptive to adopting the values and prohibitions of the caretaker, for these adoptions allow him to maintain a close attachment. If an infant becomes attached to the mother during the first year of life, he becomes anxious when she leaves. As he enters the second year and conquers his fear of being physically separated from her, fear of potential disapproval may replace the earlier fear of physical separation. The child is prone to inhibit behaviors the mother dislikes and initiate those she values. The stronger the attachment to the mother during the first year, the more motivated the child should be in gaining the approval of the mother and, subsequently, other adults.

The typical middle class mother spends dramatically more time playing and talking with her infant and allowing her infant to grasp and cling to her than does the lower class mother. Consequently, the middle class infant becomes more closely attached to the mother and is more receptive to believing in and practicing her values. Support for this position can be seen in a simple laboratory experiment. Lower-middle and upper-middle class infants, 8 months old, were first allowed to play with toys in a room with their mother present. When the child was relatively happy, the mother left the room. Upper-middle class children were more likely to cry and become upset than lower class infants.

Many lower class mothers believe, unfortunately, that there is little they can do to enhance their relationship with their child. They feel more impotent about their power to influence the child and they do not enter into long reciprocal periods of play. Middle class mothers, by contrast, play out the Pygmalion story, shaping and molding the infant to fit their ideal. This active sculpting leads the mother to engage in interactions that permit the child to develop an attachment to the parent. The zeal of the middle class first grader seems to derive, in part, from his motivation to establish a close relation to the teacher which, in turn, is a derivative of the early attachment to the mother.

Inhibition

A fourth difference between the two classes involves inhibition. The poor child shows less inhibition in times of conflict, and devotes less time to consideration of alternatives in a choice situation. In a word, the poor child tends to be impulsive. There are two possible causes for this difference. First, the mother of poverty is likely to be impulsive in her own actions and thus acts as a model for this type of behavior. Second, the poor child may not see or recognize the conflict inherent in a situation because he does not activate all the cognitive structures relevant to that problem. As a result, he behaves as though there is no choice to be made.

Sense of Effectiveness

The middle class 4-year-old seems to have a better sense of his potential effectiveness than the lower class child, who often sits withdrawn in the home, announcing his feeling of impotence as an agent who can cause things to happen. Consider a human infant 8 weeks old lying in a crib with an attractive mobile dangling 2 feet above his face. One infant can make the mobile turn by moving his head on his pillow. For a second infant the mobile moves at random, unrelated to his head movements. The first child shows more joy than the second. He babbles and smiles, while the second is quiet.

Instrumental control of the environment is a pleasant experience. The child who persists with difficult problems will more frequently enjoy the excitement that accompanies success and will develop an expectancy of success and a sense of his own effectiveness. Middle class two year olds enter into longer periods of sustained play with toys than lower class children and, hence, are more likely to successfully complete a product. Moreover, the middle class child often shows his newly built tower to a parent, expecting some positive response, and a sense of effectiveness may be influenced by parental actions toward the infant. The middle class mother who responds to her infant's smiling and cooing by talking and smiling back is laying a foundation for the belief that the child is a causal agent. The mother who comes to her child when he cries is clearly contributing to the child's faith in his ability to do something effective when he is in distress.

There are subtle accomplishments that the infant masters during the first year and a half of life that mothers can praise. The infant typically begins to smile at faces and swipe at objects at 3 to 4 months, grab at distant objects with perfect accuracy at 5 months, sit up at 7 months, stand at 11 months, and walk at 14 months. Middle class mothers often react to these attainments with peals of praise and physical affection. The future investment in mastery of new skills is aided if the child expects pleasure from the conquest, and middle class children seem to have a stronger faith in success than children of poverty.

Motivation and Expectancy of Failure

When the child reaches school age, two new differences emerge. A 7-year-old child of poverty is not highly motivated to work at school defined tasks, partly because he feels less friendly toward the teacher and does not have a strong desire to obtain her praise, and partly because he does not admire her skills or temperamental qualities. Moreover he continues to expect to fail at intellectual problems and invests less effort in their mastery or, at the extreme, avoids them completely. Failure is less humiliating for he had not expected to succeed and was not convinced that intellectual skills were valuable. The combination of inadequate language resources, low motivation, and little faith in success leads inevitably to the retarded school progress so characteristic of the lower class child.

Some Illustrations

Some illustrations may aid appreciation of these theoretical ideas. If an adult presents a difficult puzzle to a 5-year-old middle class child, he will work at the task for a minute or two and, if he cannot solve it, push it toward the adult explaining, "I can't do it," "It's too hard," or "Let's do something else." Despite failure, he makes an active response. The poor child is likely to work only 10 seconds on the problem and less likely to take responsibility for terminating this painful experience. An examiner might wait 3 or 4 minutes of interminable silence before asking, "Can you do it?" The child quietly shakes his head from side to side. This passive posture in the face of a difficult problem is not uncommon among poor children.

The middle class child also is more planful, as the following sequence illustrates. A 4-year-old girl first looked at 12 different pictures and then was asked to remember the ones she saw without looking back at the book. Most 4 year olds can remember about four pictures under these circumstances. After recalling two pictures, she told the examiner, "I think I'll just tell

you one or two more and then we'll do something else, o.k.?"
She had realized she was only able to recall two more pictures
and cleverly began to defend herself against the moment when
she had nothing more to say.

These are seven major sets of differences between young
children from families of differing economic privilege. Let us now
turn to some data which lend support to some of these
hypotheses. The major sources of data come from two studies in
our laboratory. The first is a longitudinal study of first born
white infants seen at four ages in the first 2 years of life. The
second is a cross-sectional study of ten-month-old, first born girls
from both lower and middle class families.

RESEARCH FINDINGS: A LONGITUDINAL STUDY

A group of 140 boys and girls, white and first born, ranging
from lower-middle to upper-middle class were seen in the
laboratory at 4, 8, 13, and 27 months of age and observed at
home in interaction with their mother at 4 and 27 months of age.
In one set of episodes the children were shown a set of clay
masks, like those illustrated in Fig. 1, at each of the four
assessments. We have suggested in an earlier publication (Kagan,
1969) that, after 11 to 12 months of age, duration of fixation
time to discrepant events is controlled primarily by the richness
of hypotheses activated in the service of assimilation. Long
fixations reflect persistent activation of a rich nest of hypotheses.

Changes in Fixation Time

Class differences in duration of fixation time to the masks
were minimal at 4 and 8 months, but at both 13 and 27 months
middle class children devoted a longer period of attention to
these faces than lower class children. We assume that the middle
class child had richer cognitive structures available and was more

likely to activate these structures when exposed to a discrepant event, such as the scrambled face. Second, the increase in attentiveness to these faces between 1 and 2 years of age was

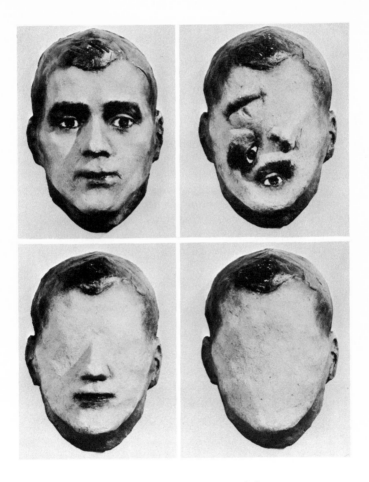

FIG. 1. Clay masks shown to infants.

more striking for the middle than for the lower class children, suggesting that the rate of acquisition of cognitive structures surrounding faces was greater for the middle class child. When the stimuli were transformations of human forms (rather than faces) there was a significant correlation between social class and duration of attention at one year ($r = .36, p < .01$ for girls; $r = .21$ for boys).

Changes in Vocalization

Nonmorphemic vocalization during the first year of life reflects, among other things, the excitement generated by an interesting event. Excitement often accompanies or follows a successful assimilation of a discrepant experience and may index the degree to which the infant is involved in the dynamic process of understanding experience. Analysis of vocalization patterns to the faces and forms presented to the longitudinal sample revealed a larger increase in vocalization for middle than for lower-middle class girls during the period from 8 to 13 months. Lower-middle class girls showed no change in vocalization across this 5-month interval; upper middle class girls displayed a 50% increase ($p < .01$ for class difference). At 27 months of age the middle class children, especially the girls, had higher vocabulary scores and showed more spontaneous verbalization.

Changes in Fear

As indicated above, the children saw clay faces at 4, 8, 13, and 27 months. At 8 months of age significantly more upper-middle than lower-middle class infants showed fearful crying to the unrealistic masks. We interpret this finding to mean that the middle class infants had a stronger need to assimilate the discrepant mask. They noted the disarranged face and tried to assimilate it to their schema for a human face. Those infants who could not accomplish this assimilation became anxious. Anxiety occurs when the child is alerted by a discrepant event, attempts to assimilate it, but is unable to do so. The lower class child, it is suggested, noted the discrepancy but was less likely to attempt the assimilation. Thus the tension born of the initial alerting dissipated and anxiety did not occur. The middle class child tried, but was unable to assimilate the scrambled face and, as a result, became anxious and cried. When the child's cognitive structures are mature enough to permit interpretation of discrepant events, fear does not appear; for no child cried when these same faces were shown to them at 27 months.

RESEARCH FINDINGS: A CROSS SECTIONAL STUDY

These class differences are supported by a more detailed cross sectional study of 60 10-month-old white girls, first born, living in the Boston-Cambridge area. Thirty of the children were middle class; 30, lower class. Middle class was defined as: either one or both parents had graduated from college and the father was at a professional job. Working class was defined as: either one or both parents had dropped out of high school and neither had attended college, or the father was working at a semiskilled or unskilled job.

Home Observations

Observations in the home were made by Steven Tulkin who supervised the study as part of his doctoral dissertation. The observer made two separate visits to the home; observational time was about 2 hours for each visit. The observer had a list of *a priori* categories for the mother and child behaviors which were coded once every 5 seconds. The primary observer taught the coding system to another female and then both visited the homes of 10 infants. Each of the 10 homes in the reliability sample was observed for 2 hours and percentages of agreement were computed for each variable. The range was 70-100%, and all median percentages were above 80%.

Laboratory Assessment

Within a few days of the home observation, the child and mother came to the laboratory. The staff who assessed the child had no knowledge of his behavior in the home and were not told about the social class of the family.

Meaningful Speech. During the first episode a tape recording of meaningful and nonmeaningful speech was played to the child. There were four stimuli in this episode: high meaningful sentences read with high or low inflection; and nonsense words read with high or low inflection. These sentences were read by two different female voices with foreign accents (one Chinese and one Spanish). Half the subjects heard one voice, the other half the second voice.

Mother's Voice. The second episode included tape recordings of the voice of the subject's mother and the voice of another subject's mother (hereafter called the stranger) reading a fairytale. Each subject heard the voice of a different stranger from her own group, either middle class or lower class. As in the first set of auditory stimuli, the passages were 20 seconds long and separated by a 10 second interstimulus interval. All the children heard the passages in the same order.

Play Behavior. Following two other episodes, not described here, mother and infant were taken to another part of the building to a carpeted room 9½ X 11½ feet square. Initially the child was given a 2-minute adaptation period designed to accustom him to the room. Three single toys were presented succeeding each other, each for 4 minutes. After the child had played with each toy for 4 minutes, two conflict trials were presented. Each conflict trial was 4 minutes in length and consisted of presenting one of the single toys simultaneous with a new toy the child had not seen previously. The two toys were presented equidistant from the child and about 2 feet apart.

Maternal Behavior in the Home

The statistically significant differences between the lower and middle class mothers involved vocalization and duration of interactive episodes. The middle class mother spent more time in a face-to-face posture with the infant, more time talking to her infant, usually within 2 feet of the infant's face, and issued more distinctive vocalization to the infant. A distinctive vocalization was coded when the mother was talking to her infant in a face-to-face position but was not providing any other sensory input, either visual or tactile. This last result replicates a similar class difference observed in mothers of 4-month-old infants.

The middle class mothers were more likely to entertain their children with objects, to encourage walking, and to reward them for mastery. However, there were no class differences for kissing, total holding of the infant, tickling and bouncing of the infant, nonverbal interaction, or verbal prohibitions. The higher rate of vocalization among middle class mothers held not only for vocalizations that were reactions to the infant's babbling, but also for spontaneously initiated verbalizations toward the infant.

Infant Behavior in the Laboratory

Meaningful vs. Nonmeaningful Speech. There were no class differences in absolute reactivity to each of the stimuli. However, when one compared the reaction to the most meaningful stimulus (high meaning-high inflection) with reactivity to the preceding stimulus (low meaning-high inflection) class differences emerged. Middle class, in contrast to lower class, infants quieted more dramatically to high meaning-high inflection than to the preceding stimulus ($p < .05$), and were more likely to look at the stranger following termination of high meaning-high inflection ($p < .10$). Most infants looked at the stranger following termination of the first stimulus, but this interest gradually waned. When high meaning-high inflection occurred on the fourth trial the middle class infants increased their orientation to the stranger, while lower class subjects did not, suggesting either that the middle class infant was better able to differentiate meaningful from nonmeaningful speech, or was more likely to inquire about the source of the meaningful speech. We shall return to this possibility later.

Mother's Voice vs. Stranger's Voice. There were no significant class differences in the mean scores for each of the variables considered separately, but the second order differences differentiated the classes. Middle class infants quieted more to mother's voice than to stranger's voice, and, upon termination of the voice, vocalized more following mother than stranger. Comparisons between the classes were both significant ($p < .05$ for quieting and $p < .10$ for vocalizing following the passages). Further, middle class infants looked at the mother following termination of her voice and looked at the stranger following termination of the stranger's voice. Working class children gradually habituated their orientation to the mother over the first four stimuli, but showed increased looking at the stranger. However, the "looking" was not related to the voice they had just heard. Moreover, the middle class infants who looked more at their mother following the termination of the mother's voice had quieted more while listening to the mother's voice ($r = .32$, $p < .10$). This class difference may mean either that the lower class girls did not recognize the difference between the two voices or did not care to inquire about the sources of the voices.

Our preferred interpretation is that all the infants were alerted by the acoustic differences between the two voices. The middle class infant wanted to resolve the discrepancy and to determine, if possible, the source of the voices. The lower class children did not have this mental set.

Play Behavior. The play session revealed no class differences for mobility, proximity to mother, or duration of play with the toys. There was, however, a difference on the conflict trials. Middle class subjects showed more vacillation before they made their final choice of toy. The middle class subjects shifted their gaze about 2.2 times, in contrast to 1.4 for the lower class subjects. We interpret this difference to reflect a tendency to retrieve past experience in the service of resolving discrepancy.

An unusual event tends to provoke an infant to attempt assimilation in order to reach cognitive equilibrium. The pairing of a novel and familiar toy is an "odd event," but children differ in their need to assimilate this discrepancy and, therefore, in the disposition to retrieve the relevant cognitive structures that might aid assimilation. This interpretation resembles the one used to explain the differences between middle and lower class infants on the two auditory episodes. We recognize the conjectural nature of this interpretation, but note the provocative implication that a primary difference between middle and lower class children may rest in their desire to understand discrepant experience.

CONCLUSION AND COMMENT

These data, although provocative, are still too thin a base to rationalize the theoretical ideas suggested earlier. However, these observations are consistent with those ideas. Although we are arguing for changes in the mother-infant relationship, these changes may only help the child's growth during the first 2-2½ years. They will not have a continuing beneficial effect if no other changes occur in the child's ecology as he enters the preschool years.

There must be a concerted effort on the part of social scientists, urban planners, and politicians to change the conditions under which poor families live. The communities' belief as to what arrangements will help them is critical. Even in psychotherapy we know that the patient does not improve if he does not believe the doctor's diagnoses and has no faith in his suggestions for cure. A sense of control over one's future and a stake in the next day are likely to develop if the parent *believes* that a specific set of changes in daily practices is reasonable and the parent knows that he or she has the option to choose the procedures. It is more important for a mother to believe that a particular alteration in her practices or life space will help, regardless of the theoretical validity of the change, than to have imposed upon her a set of interventions in which she has no faith. An imposed procedure that does not engage a commitment in its effectiveness is not likely to do much good. Each community must be allowed to participate in the arrangements for its living.

Man is neither evil nor insane enough to invent completely toxic conditions for the care of children. The poor mother is deeply concerned about the welfare of her child. She must be helped to feel that she can implement her concern through exposure to caretaking practices that make sense to her as well as the psychologist.

ACKNOWLEDGMENTS

The research was supported in part by grants HD 4299 from NICHD, USPHS, and the Carnegie Corporation of New York.

REFERENCES

Kagan, J. On the meaning of behavior: Illustrations from the infant. *Child Development,* 1969, **40**, 1121-1134.

Chapter 3

Early Deprivation in Biological Perspective | *William A. Mason*

A biological perspective on early deprivation implies a concern with animal research, with comparative studies, and with the evolution of behavior. My task is to apply this perspective to problems of human education. With so many urgent practical problems pressing for solution, one might very well ask whether a biological perspective on human education is necessary, or, for that matter, even useful. The problems are obvious, it would seem, and so are the solutions. All that is required is the right people, with the right plans, and the wherewithal to carry them out.

If this attitude prevails, then the suggestion that a link exists between biology and education is apt to strike as another of those pious truths of dubious relevance to the practical affairs of contemporary society. Needless to say, I do not share this view. I doubt that the problems we face are all that self-evident; I question that the proposed solutions are uniformly sound; and I am convinced that the issues are of such transcendent importance that we cannot afford to bypass any avenue that offers some hope of advance.

What can a biological perspective contribute to the question of human education? It can contribute at least two things. First, it can contribute a necessary corrective to the thoroughly lop-sided view that man has risen so far above his humble origins that he can afford to ignore them altogether, the view that what he *is* can be properly reckoned without taking into account how he *came to be.* We like to see ourselves as creatures no longer required to adapt to the environment in which we have evolved, but instead adapting the environment to suit our purposes. We are the biologically elite; the managers of this whole vast earthly enterprise. And the world shall be as we wish it. This is at best a half-truth and at worst a case of galloping arrogance of frightening proportions. The more sobering consequences of accepting this narrow anthropocentric conceit are becoming more apparent each day, as we are confronted with further evidence of our marvelous ingenuity in devising new ways to foul our nest. We need a corrective to our one-sided view of man as manager, a view in which the idea of stewardship is also present. And we need to see ourselves more clearly as a part and a product of the world we plunder and pollute.

And with particular reference to the theme of this work, we need to try to see human intelligence—the major instrument of our accomplishments and our difficulties as a species—in a broader and more natural context. Human intelligence, like everything else about the human organism, is an evolutionary achievement. It is an achievement of spectacular proportions, to be sure, but it began as a response to problems that are far older than man and it is built on ancient foundations.

This is not to say that *Homo sapiens* does not have impressive claims to uniqueness. The humanist is certainly correct to insist that human affairs belong in a class all their own. There is no reason to quibble about this. But then if the dolphin were gifted with the powers of speech (and some have come close to maintaining that he is), could he not advance the same claims for the affairs of dolphins? Or for that matter could not the wolf, or the chimpanzee? My point, obviously, is that biological unique-ness is not limited to man, and the claim of uniqueness provides no sufficient grounds for dealing with man as a creature apart. What are the terms of his uniqueness? What is its source and nature? And what does man share in common with other creatures of the earth? I think you will agree that if we are truly concerned with discovering wherein our uniqueness lies, we have no choice but to adopt a biological perspective.

The second contribution that a biological perspective can make to our understanding of human education is heuristic. And by that I mean that what is discovered through research on animals can serve as a guide and a stimulus to thinking and planning about human problems. What is the nature of intelligence and how can we make it grow and prosper? No educational enterprise—no matter how practical and down-to-earth its immediate goals might be—can avoid coming to grips with this issue. Any training program must make assumptions about what intelligence is and the conditions appropriate to its full and effective development. What is the proper age to begin instruction? Are some tasks beyond the capabilities of a given age group? What assurances do we have that opportunities missed early in life can be made up for at later ages? In asking these questions we imply certain assumptions about what intelligence is and how it works.

But the critic will surely reply that we can answer the questions without examining the underlying assumptions. He will insist that we can get on with practical matters without bothering ourselves with tedious experiments on animals and biological speculations. And, up to a point, he is certainly right. But there are risks. Intelligence is not a thing, but a function; it is a way of dealing with the world. And the only way you can explore a function is to tinker with it. If one wants to find out the conditions under which it works well, one can hardly avoid the possibility that conditions will be created under which it works less well—is perhaps even seriously impaired. Furthermore, without some understanding of what it is we are tampering with, we run the risk of never knowing why, in any particular instance, our efforts succeed or fail. These inevitable risks provide the major practical justification for extracting whatever heuristic aid we can from research on animals.

There is, indeed, a growing awareness that a biological

perspective can help to clarify our assumptions about the nature and nurture of human intelligence. In fact, it is fair to say that many of the important changes in our views of intelligence that have come about within the last decade or so, can be attributed to new insights growing out of animal research (e.g., Hayes, 1962; Hunt, 1961). My purpose here is to describe some of these changes, to indicate the kinds of evidence that have brought them about, and to consider some of the implications for human education.

INTELLIGENCE IN BIOLOGICAL PERSPECTIVE

What is intelligence as viewed from a biological perspective? Like all important evolutionary innovations, intelligence has arisen out of the need to deal with change. It is a way of bringing about a better fit between the vital needs of the organism and the inescapable requirements that the environment imposes.

The distinctive attribute of intelligence, of course, is that the organism adjusts to change by doing something as a whole; it takes some action, such as moving to another place, pushing something aside, or going round a barrier. Intelligence implies a behaving organism, behavior implies information processing. Consider a little more carefully what this means. A behaving organism must be able to accomplish four things: It must be able to select certain "relevant" segments from the total array of environmental energies; to encode this energy; to use the resulting information as the basis for elaborating some course of action; and to act on the information received. In other words, the behaving animal is prepared to detect only certain environmental events; it must translate these events into the "language" of the nervous system, decide what to do about the message, and take some action. From this point of view, even the simplest kind of behavior is the external manifestation of a more complex information processing system—a system whose main business is the evaluation of environmental contingencies and the selection of appropriate responses.

For such a system to be workable and biologically useful it must possess two characteristics: First, it must provide some form of internal representation of the order and the regularities in the environment (von Foerster, 1968). The behaving organism requires an *image* of the world—an image in the sense that the information it acts on and the action it takes are consistent with the structure of the environment. The image need not be pictorial, of course, nor need we assume that all organisms have similar images, in complexity or kind; in fact, we can be certain they do not. The important point is that animals are equipped with functional representations of the world, or schemas, and these schemas must, more often than not, correspond with the exigencies and constraints that the environment imposes. Second, the system must point ahead; it requires a predictive or probabilistic component (Bjorkman, 1966; Brunswik, 1955). The toad's tongue flicking out toward a small spot moving into its visual field is a reaction to the "probability" that it will encounter something good to eat. Likewise, the monkey's leap from one tree to another implies a certain "confidence" in the weight-bearing potential of tree limbs, the reliability of distance cues, and so on. Information processing must be predictive because the pay-off always lies ahead. The adaptiveness of any action will depend upon its consequences; it can only be determined after the fact.

Every response can thus be seen as an act of faith. Faith that the information received is trustworthy; and faith that the course of action selected will be "correct." From this point of view the toad and the monkey have much in common. Both operate on the basis of schematic representations of the environment. Both are always and of necessity playing the odds. They must treat the information they receive as reliable—as an honest tender of the world as it really is—and they must use the information received to select some program of action as the most likely to result in success. Both can make mistakes. The toad may seize a noxious object; the monkey's leap could send it crashing to the ground.

In the long run, however, the response is usually "correct"; its consequences are beneficial. In principle, of course, there is nothing mysterious about how this has come about. There is no need to endow either the toad or the monkey with a crystal ball, nor with even the dimmest understanding of probability theory. The principles of natural selection are fully capable of explaining how it is that behavior is both representational and predictive. The species that is too often deceived by its senses or too often errs in its selection of responses is on the road to certain extinction.

PHYLETIC CONTRASTS

But if schemas provide the basic framework of intelligent behavior, how do we account for the obvious fact that some species are so much more intelligent than others? Why is a monkey so much smarter than a toad and yet not nearly so bright as even a rather dull-witted man? Quite possibly, the toad, the monkey, and the man have different schemas. I would like to suggest an additional possibility, however, which may have a more fundamental bearing on questions of the evolution of intelligence. I believe that one of the great differences between the toad, the monkey, and the man will be found in the "openness" of their schemas. By "openness" I refer to the ease with which schemas can be modified by experience, the extent to which they can incorporate new information. It is no accident, I believe, that the emergence of "intelligence" and the degeneration of "instincts" have gone hand-in-hand in animal evolution; intelligence is the result of a transformation of primordial schemas—inherent species-typical modes of information processing—in the direction of greater openness, and consequently, of greater behavioral flexibility. (For similar views see Kuttner, 1960; Lashley, 1949; Stenhouse, 1965.)

Three different aspects of openness can be distinguished on logical grounds and are readily demonstrated empirically. They relate to the collection of information (the receptor side of behavior), the flexibility or versatility of motor acts (the effector side), and what goes on in between receiving and acting (the processing of information).

Increased Sensory Differentiation

With regard to the collection of information, two rather different functions can be discerned which have contributed to increased openness and I have included both under the heading of sensory differentiation. The "open" organism is able to respond to many different aspects of any given situation. The range of effective stimuli is broader, and at the same time, minor variations in the situation are less important. It is as though the open organism were better able to see the trees *and* the forest, to comprehend the parts and their relation to the whole.

Again the toad can be instructive, this time to help clarify what sensory differentiation involves. The toad is an animal with very limited capabilities for the differentiation of food stimuli. For the toad, "food" is any small object moving into his visual field; his food-catching program is activated by that event. There are two obvious limitations in this program. One is that any moving object is responded to as food, whether it is edible or not. The other is that if an object does not move, it is not food, and a toad can starve to death surrounded by immobile but perfectly nutritious flies (Kaess & Kaess, 1960). One might say that for the toad there is no forest of edible objects, only trees, and all trees look alike.

It should be emphasized here that openness is always a question of degree. Even the toad is not entirely without resources for modifying its prey-catching schema in the face of new information. If a red ant is substituted for the fly, the snapping response is inhibited after a few feeding attempts, although the effect is only transitory (Maier & Schneirla, 1935; Noble, 1931). It might also be pointed out that openness varies not only with phylogeny, but with the particular schema. The eye-blink response to a rapidly approaching object is an example of a relatively closed schema in man. This response appears early in ontogeny and persists throughout life with little apparent change. It can be modified, of course, we can inhibit the response, but only with difficulty, a property which has made it a suitable object for a familiar children's game.

Increased Differentiation of Motor Acts

Another aspect of openness is illustrated by the familiar saying that there is more than one way to skin a cat. For less intelligent organisms this saying is often not true. The goose retrieving an egg that has rolled out of her nest, for example, knows only one way to skin the cat. If she happens to notice the egg outside the nest, she stares at it awhile, then she approaches it, faces it, and placing her bill on the far side of the egg rolls it toward her feet (and the nest). All this is done in a highly stereotyped pattern of movements, and if the egg happens to roll to one side and slips from beneath her bill, she may continue right on with the movement just as though nothing had changed; or she may break off and later start the entire sequence from the beginning. If the nest is so situated that the egg cannot be returned in this manner, it is eventually lost. Although the goose's wings and feet are seemingly much better suited to the job of rolling eggs into a nest, they are never used for this purpose (Lorenz & Tinbergen, 1957; Tinbergen, 1950).

Now consider an analogous example in a more "intelligent" form, a nonhuman primate. The South American squirrel monkey is certainly not the most generously endowed mother among the nonhuman primates. In fact, for a monkey, she is unusually passive in her approach to infant care. Modest as her achievements are, however, she is far removed from the goose. Under ordinary circumstances the mother squirrel monkey rarely handles her baby or cradles it to her breast, even during feeding. If she happens to become separated from her infant, she retrieves it by hovering over it until it grabs her fur and climbs aboard. Under ordinary circumstances there is no need for more elaborate behavior since from the first day of life the infant is able to cling to the mother without her help, to move about on her body and to find the nipple and suckle unassisted. However, if the infant is unable to cling because it is weak or its arms have been restrained, the mother abandons her customary passive role, actively retrieves the infant and carries it in her arms (Rumbaugh, 1965).

This is perhaps the place to emphasize that I am not talking about differences between what is "learned" and what is "innate." Nothing that the monkey mother does when she picks up her disabled infant is really new. The motor patterns have been there all the time. Nor do I have any doubt that the goose has all the effector equipment she needs to use her feet or wings instead of her beak to maneuver wayward eggs into her nest. It is the monkey's ability to call upon different motor patterns as circumstances require that distinguishes her retrieving behavior from that of the goose. For all we know, the behavior of both animals may be under the control of a superordinate "maternal instinct," but the greater flexibility of the squirrel monkey's motor patterns allows her to perform her maternal activities in a more intelligent manner.

Increased Integrative Capacities.

Some of the most significant, complex, and elusive functions underlying intelligent behavior have to do with the integration or processing of information—the events that occur between the stimulus and the response. Included here are the capabilities for putting together information from different sensory modalities, or from the same modality at different points in time, for abstracting, generalizing, and forming rules and strategies on the basis of prior experience. What makes such functions possible is by no means certain, but that they do occur, and that they occur not only in man and his closer biological kin, is established, I believe, beyond any reasonable doubt.

One important implication of this kind of openness is that it permits schemas to be built up or elaborated as development proceeds. Thus, the newborn rhesus monkey begins life with a schematic mother which is a very incomplete representation of monkey mothers as we know them. In the beginning the defining properties of "mother" are almost entirely tactile, and the infant will accept, cling to, and eventually form an emotional attachment to blankets, diapers, terrycloth towels, and a host of other biologically improbable objects (Harlow & Zimmermann, 1958). In some respects the monkey's schematic mother is as meager as the toad's schematic food object. In contrast to the toad, however, the monkey's primitive schema undergoes a rapid and progressive enrichment as new information is incorporated into the system. As physical attributes and their arrangements in space and time become associated with a single source, "mother" emerges as an entity; she acquires object status. Eventually she is recognized from a distance and from various angles of regard. Her distinctive physical attributes combine with a vast number of more dynamic features that help to define the relationship between mother and child. The growing monkey ultimately arrives at a conception of "mother" which in subtlety and complexity must rival our own.

Another implication of improved capacities for integrating information is greater facility in adjusting to radical changes in the normal relations between input and effector patterns. An illustration of this facility can be found in the contrasting reactions of amphibians and primates to imposed rearrangement of the visual field. The frog that has had its eyes rotated 180 degrees, strikes just 180 degrees off target and it will persist indefinitely in this maladaptive response. A similar condition can be imposed on monkey or man by the use of inversion lenses. When this is done they also have great difficulty adjusting to the change initially, but they improve rapidly and within a few days are able to get around with reasonable skill (Foley, 1940; Sperry, 1951; Stratton, 1897).

DEPRIVATION EFFECTS

More open schemas confer some obvious biological advantages, but they also entail some risks. Increased openness means greater flexibility but it also means that initial schemas are often functionally unstable, if not incomplete. Open schemas presumably require input as a source of stability and a means of filling "gaps." If this is true, we would anticipate that the "open" organism deprived of certain critical experiences early in life will be seriously handicapped in its later adjustments. This expectation is amply confirmed by the available evidence; some of the specific deficiencies and aberrations that have appeared in animals as a consequence of early deprivation will be considered in this chapter. The effects range from degenerative changes, impairments and distortions in primitive schemas, through susceptibility to overload and deficient problem-solving skills, to curtailed development of higher-order functions. Although no sharp distinction can be made between these different effects, it is probably true that the order given is roughly hierarchical in the sense that the effects that appear earlier on the list do not occur without those that appear later, whereas the converse does not hold. Thus, degenerative changes preclude the development of some higher-order functions, but the absence of higher-order functions does not imply the presence of degenerative processes.

Breakdown of Primordial Schemas

It now appears certain that some primitive schemas, present and ready to operate essentially at birth, lose this capability in the absence of appropriate input. For example, withholding visual stimulation brings about structural and biochemical changes in the retina, cellular changes in the visual fields of the central nervous system, various oculomotor abnormalities such as chronic nystagmus and strabismus, and, as would be expected, serious and persistent deficiencies in a great many behavioral adjustments mediated by the visual system. Radical deprivation can thus lead not merely to developmental arrest, but to functional disintegration of established systems. (For reviews see Riesen, 1966; Teuber, 1967.)

Lack of Environmental "Tuning"

There are also strong indications from recent research that many of the basic sensory-motor skills that we are likely to take for granted do not function adequately until some opportunity for normal use is provided. Some of the most convincing demonstrations of this point have been provided by Richard Held and his associates in their research on the genesis of visuomotor coordinations. In one experiment, for example, kittens were raised in the dark except for a brief daily period of controlled exposure in a lighted chamber. During this exposure period one group of kittens was permitted to locomote more or less freely, whereas the second group was restrained in a gondola and moved passively about the chamber. The passive kittens thus received essentially the same visual stimulation as the active kittens, but, unlike the active kittens, they had no opportunity to integrate visual information with their walking movements. Subsequent tests indicated that the active kittens showed normal behavior in visually guided tasks. They blinked at approaching objects, extended their forepaws to ward off an impending collision, and gave other evidence of adequate depth perception. In contrast, the passive kittens failed to show these behaviors until they were given the opportunity to move about freely within a normal environment (Held, 1965; Held & Hein, 1963). In another experiment infant macaque monkeys were raised from birth in a situation which prevented them from seeing their own hands. When tested at 35 days of age for accuracy of reaching toward a visible object, they were inferior to control monkeys of the same age (Held & Bauer, 1967). The basic schema for eye-hand coordination seemed to be present, as evidenced by the fact that reaching in the general direction of the object occurred almost from the beginning, and by the finding that with opportunity for rehearsal and "self-instruction" the accuracy of performance improved noticeably within a matter of hours. However, the precise tuning of the program required the specific experience of viewing the moving hand.

A preliminary phase of sensory-motor tuning is no doubt a prerequisite for the development of more complex skills. Birch's observations on the use of tools by chimpanzees is clearly pertinent here (Birch, 1945). He found that animals that consistently failed to solve relatively simple stick-using tasks showed a dramatic improvement in performance after they had been given an opportunity for casual play with sticks. In the course of this activity the chimps gradually fitted the sticks into their existing reaching patterns and came to use them as functional extensions of the arm. Once this functional connection had been established the focus of the animal's attention seemed to shift toward exploring the other specialized properties "inherent" in the stick-as-object. The higher levels of performance are thus built upon the simpler achievements that precede them (see also Menzel, Davenport, & Rogers, 1970). A similar process is probably at work in the development of certain social patterns. For example, I suspect that lack of opportunity for sensory-motor tuning is a significant factor in the sexual deficiencies of socially deprived rhesus males. Most of the components of the complete sex act are present in these animals, but because of inadequate opportunity for rehearsal the elements have not become integrated into a biologically effective pattern (Mason, 1960).

Distortion of Schemas

From a structural point of view schemas are inherent, species-typical tendencies toward organizing experience in certain ways. As we have seen, withholding information early in life may cause degenerative changes in these structures or interfere with precision tuning. Recent findings also suggest that schemas may continue to influence development in circumstances in which the usual environmental supports and constraints are eliminated. Under such circumstances aberrant patterns can emerge—behaviors that are quite outside the normal range of variation and reflect the particular conditions of the rearing environment. The result is not behavioral disorganization, but a deviant pattern produced by the interplay between atypical input and intrinsic schemas.

Perhaps the clearest examples of such interactions are provided by the acquisition of song by birds. Some birds such as the Indian Hill Mynah show a remarkable capacity to acquire new sound patterns, whereas others display practically no talent for picking up songs. The most instructive species are those that fall somewhere between these extremes. In these birds the full development of the species-typical song is dependent upon hearing other birds sing; and the individual that is deprived of this experience develops an abnormal song pattern, usually simpler than the full song typical of the species. Although the bird may be said to acquire its song, it often displays a definite predilection for certain song patterns. For example, Chaffinches exposed to the songs of many different species, acquire the song that comes closest to the normal song of their species (Marler & Hamilton, 1966; Thorpe, 1956).

A similar selective process is suggested by some of the self-directed behaviors that appear in many nonhuman primates raised apart from the mother. Such animals frequently suck their fingers or toes and clasp themselves, particularly when they are emotionally distressed (e.g., Mason & Green, 1962). These behaviors have clear counterparts, of course, in responses usually directed toward the mother. Because the infant monkey or ape raised alone in a bare cage fails to encounter the normal outlets for clinging and sucking, he presumably directs these responses toward the most accessible and appropriate materials that are available and these happen to be parts of its own body. The organizing effects of intrinsic schemas are also suggested by some of the self-directed responses that appear during later phases of primate development, such as the self-biting and genital stimulation often shown by isolation-reared adolescent monkeys and apes. For example, the young rhesus male often thrusts against its leg when sexually aroused, even though genital stimulation could seemingly be accomplished more effectively by other means. Sexual arousal apparently activates a particular sensory motor schema which in the course of its development has become adapted to the special circumstances of the rearing environment.

Excessive Arousal Effects

Another reliable consequence of early deprivation is a tendency toward fearfulness or heightened emotionality. The behavioral expressions of this effect are quite varied, and depend on the particular species, as well as the situation in which the animal is observed. Motor discharge may take an exaggerated form, as in seizures, tics, whirling fits or frantic running, or it may be minimal, as in crouching, freezing, fainting, or falling to sleep (Riesen, 1961).

It might be argued that these behaviors result from a breakdown in the processing of information, caused by overload on systems whose development has been curtailed by early restrictions on experience. The deprived organism is ill-equipped to deal with unfamiliar input, with complexity, and with change. It is deficient in the ability to assimilate new information—an ability that the normal animal has been exercising almost continuously since early infancy—and it responds to new situations with seizures, tics, and freezing, presumably because it is overwhelmed by the sudden increase in stimulation, and has no other means of coping with it.

Recently, Melzack has proposed a neurological model which deals explicitly with the relation between deficiencies in information processing and excessive arousal (Melzack, 1965, 1968; Melzack & Burns, 1965). Melzack regards sensory input as a two-part process in which activation (or arousal) and stimulus selection are treated as separate functions. Neurophysiological findings suggest that afferent fibers can be divided into "fast" and "slow" on the basis of conduction rates. These two classes are assumed to serve different functions. The fast fibers activate processes in the central nervous system (such processes would be schemas in our terminology) which subserve memory, attention, and similar functions. When activated these systems feed back on lower synaptic levels where they can inhibit, facilitate, or otherwise modify the input patterns of the more slowly conducting afferent fibers. In this fashion they exert active control over the selection of information.

As the result of sensory restriction, the development of these central nervous system processes is impaired. The selection of relevant information and the filtering out of irrelevant information is faulty; the loss of filtering leads to diffuse bombardment of the central nervous system, one consequence of which is excessive arousal. This state of affairs traps the animal in a vicious circle in which the cause is perpetuated by its effects: Lack of experience engenders excessive arousal; and excessive arousal disrupts the activities of the very mechanisms in the central nervous system whose further development is required for orderly and efficient information processing.

Neurophysiological speculations aside, recent experience leaves no serious doubt that the heightened emotional responsiveness of the deprived organism is a persistent liability. It can be ameliorated by subsequent treatment (e.g., Fuller, 1967), but probably never completely overcome. The electroencephalograms of isolation-reared dogs show signs of high arousal for at least 6 months after the animals are released from restriction, and behavioral indications of elevated arousal persist in deprived monkeys and apes throughout years of postrearing exposure to the normal laboratory environment (Cross & Harlow, 1965; Davenport & Rogers, 1968; Mason & Sponholz, 1963; Melzack & Burns, 1965; Sackett, 1967).

Deficiencies in Problem-Solving Skills

We know that many mammals spend much of their time actively exploring their surroundings, and this behavior is particularly prominent when some element of novelty is present (for reviews see Berlyne, 1966; Butler, 1960; Welker, 1961). We would anticipate that one of the things that is accomplished during these activities is that the animal becomes accustomed to the novel element. As it explores, it transforms the strange into the familiar. In addition to this, however, a great deal of evidence indicates that it is also acquiring information about the environment. It is learning rather specific skills that can be applied to similar situations on some future occasion in which important consequences are involved.

For example, rats raised in cages containing barriers, tunnels and playthings generally turn out to be better maze runners than rats that have not been exposed to such an "enriched" environment (e.g., Forgays & Forgays, 1952; Forgus, 1954; Hymovitch, 1952). Their "casual" experience pays off when they are required to solve a problem for food reward. Similar findings have been obtained on dogs (Fuller, 1967; Melzack, 1965; Thompson & Heron, 1954), cats (Wilson, Warren, & Abbott, 1965), and primates. A recent study conducted by Mr. Paul Anastasiou at the Delta Primate Center compared 14 laboratory-reared adolescent rhesus monkeys with an adolescent and an adult group, both born in the wild. The problems, designed to assess a variety of cognitive skills, ranged from a simple visual-search task to complex puzzle devices. The results demonstrate that both wild-born groups were unequivocally superior to either laboratory group; indeed, there was scarcely any overlap between them. The best of 14 laboratory-reared animals was about on a par with the worst of the 13 wild-born monkeys.

A recent study with chimpanzees suggests that early experience may have an enduring effect on problem-solving skills, as measured by the delayed response test (Davenport & Rogers,

1968). In this test the animal is shown the location of a piece of food and is required to find it after a short delay. In the chimp study, one group of animals was raised in enclosed cubicles for the first two years of life. After two years of isolation they were exposed to a great many different experiences, including extended periods of group-living in large outdoor enclosures. The second group of chimps was jungle-born and had been brought into the laboratory when about 2 years old. Both groups were about 7-9 years old at the time of testing. Even though the essential difference in the background of the two groups occurred only during the first 2 years of life, about 5 years before the present tests were made, it had a large impact on later performance. At all levels of delay, the isolation-reared animals were inferior to the jungle-born chimpanzees, and the differences on the longer delays persisted throughout testing. There was some indication that poor attention was one factor in this result. At the longer intervals especially, the isolation-reared animals were slow to respond at the end of the delay period, suggesting that they had difficulty maintaining a consistent orientation toward the relevant aspects of the problem. The same isolation-reared subjects were also inferior to wild-born animals in the acquisition of a discrimination learning-set (see below). Again, difficulty in attending to the relevant features of the problem seemed to be a significant factor in their poor performance (Davenport, Rogers, & Menzel, 1969).

Curtailment of Higher-Order Functions

One of the properties of open schemas is that they develop cumulatively and can be built up or elaborated as development proceeds. This characteristic was illustrated earlier by the gradual enrichment and extension of the infant rhesus monkey's "concept" of its mother. In addition to this mode of schematic growth, however, development can also lead to the establishment of new levels of organization and higher orders of control.

Hierarchical arrangements are a common feature of animal behavior. Walking, for example, which in itself is a highly organized activity, comes under the control of various "higher" centers, as in hunting, mating, or fleeing from a predator. Since the presence of such hierarchies is one of the hallmarks of intelligent behavior, it is important for us to know how they are formed.

One of the most significant contributions of animal research in recent years is the demonstration that the achievment of higher levels of control is dependent upon experiences of a specific kind and amount. A classic example of the development of a higher-order function is provided by Harlow's research on learning-set (Harlow, 1949). Harlow found that if a monkey encounters a particular type of problem-solving situation repeatedly, he learns how to learn problems of that type, seemingly by developing rules or strategies. In a typical learning-set experiment the animal is presented with a series of two-object discrimination problems, each problem for a fixed number of trials (usually about six). The monkey's task is to discover which of the two objects covers a food reward. On any single problem the animal can learn which is the correct object, of course, by the relatively inefficient process of trial and error. In fact, Harlow found that performance on the first problems was of the trial-and-error sort. As the animal gained further experience with discrimination problems, however, it required fewer trials to solve a new problem and eventually was able to solve most problems after a single information trial. The monkey had apparently shifted from trial-and-error learning to insightful solutions. It was as though it had acquired a kind of rule or strategy for solving two-object discrimination problem: Stay with the rewarded object and abandon the unrewarded, or more briefly, win-stay, lose-shift.

The learning-set procedure has provided a useful tool to comparative psychologists, and one of the more interesting discoveries to emerge from their studies is that the capacity to form discrimination learning-sets is related in orderly fashion to phyletic standing, at least within the vertebrate series. Rats and squirrels, for example, develop learning-sets more slowly and achieve a lower level of terminal performance than cats or monkeys. And both these species, of course, are inferior to man (Warren, 1965).

However, it does not follow from these important findings that the development of all higher-order functions is dependent on a single, unitary process. According to one recent estimate, human intelligence comprises as many as 120 unique abilities (Guilford, 1968). There is every reason to suppose that the intelligence of animals is also based on many abilities. But the abilities are not precisely the same in form or number as those found in man. Moreover, it is clear that certain higher-order functions are species-specific, as is the case with language in man. No doubt other animals also have their unique abilities and highly specialized skills.

In the examples we have considered thus far, rather formal training procedures were required to create higher-order functions, but this is not always the case. A recent experiment by Dr. Gordon Gallup shows that sometimes nothing more is required than an appropriate opportunity in order for a higher-order function to emerge. Gallup's experiment asked whether animals other than man can develop a "concept of self" (Gallup, 1970). His approach was based on the well-known finding that many primates respond to their images in a mirror as though they were seeing other animals. Will an animal eventually learn that the image it perceives is actually itself? To investigate this question he used both chimpanzees and macaque monkeys. On their first encounter with the mirror both species responded as though the image were another animal. The difference was that the monkeys continued to react to the mirror as if to another monkey throughout a long series of exposures, while for the chimps, social response gradually gave way to self-directed behaviors. They used the mirror as a visual aid to groom parts of their body that were otherwise inaccessible, to pick bits of food from between their teeth, and to make faces at themselves. To make sure that the chimps had come to recognize themselves in the mirror, Gallup anesthetized his animals and while they were knocked out, he painted red spots on their ears and eyebrows. After they had fully recovered from the anesthetic, the animals were again exposed to the mirror. The chimps not only spent more time viewing the mirror, but, in addition, much of their behavior was directed toward their new red spots. Although treated in the same manner as the chimpanzees, the monkeys still showed no evidence of self-recognition and continued to respond to the altered image just as though it were another monkey. Any doubt that exposure to the mirror was necessary for the development of self-recognition was eliminated by a control series in which some chimpanzees were marked before their first experience with the mirror. Like the experienced monkeys, and unlike the experienced chimps, they responded to the image as to another animal. The results show that a visual self-concept must be achieved, and that it requires certain environmental conditions in order to emerge.

Although the evidence is clear that the biological potential for the development of higher-order schemas—rules, concepts, strategies—is related to phylogeny, there is no way of anticipating on logical or intuitive grounds the specific nature of the potentialities that a given individual or species may posses. This can only be determined empirically and until it has been determined we are left with only a vague, generalized, and very unsatisfying understanding of potential achievements. Although we can be sure that the fabled horde of monkeys pounding away at their typewriters will never produce a single sonnet, we are still a long way from appreciating just how far they can go. What seems certain, however, is that for the monkey, as for man, the translation of potential abilities into concrete achievements will be intimately dependent upon specific opportunities and training experiences that it encounters.

IMPLICATIONS

This final section will attempt to sharpen the relevance of a biological perspective to problems of human education. One of my aims has been to establish the fundamental affinities between intelligence and other forms of adaptive behavior. I have emphasized that some form of internal representation of the environment is a universal requirement among behaving organisms. All are forced to treat the information they receive as reliable, and they must use it to select some program of action as the most likely to result in success. In response to this need, all have evolved various systems for the processing of information.

We have found no evidence that a sharp line can be drawn between the information processing systems involved in so-called "instinctive" and "intelligent" behaviors. I have tried to show that what most distinguishes the intelligent from the instinctive organism is the degree of openness of their information processing systems. Openness means adaptive variability, the capacity to treat different stimuli as equivalent, and to respond to the same stimulus in more than one way. Openness means moving away from rigid connections between stimulus and response and it creates the possibility that higher-order functions can be built upon more primitive structural foundations.

Although little explicit reference to learning has been made, it will be obvious that the present view assigns learning a critical part in psychological development. Its importance is greatest, of course, among strongly open organisms, such as man. Even here, however, most learning occurs within the framework of existing schemas. As Karl Lashley put it some 20 years ago, the nervous system is not a neutral medium on which learning can impose any form of organization whatever. On the contrary, it has definite predilections for certain forms of organization which it imposes on the sensory impulses that reach it (Lashley, 1949). These organizational patterns, or schemas, are the basic operating structures upon which new information acts and within which new information is fitted. Learning is guided by these structures, and it is a primary agent in their transformation from phylogenetic "plans" into adaptive functional patterns. One might speculate that the learning process has evolved as handmaiden of the instincts and that even in man, the most open of open organisms, it has not yet achieved full emancipation from this ancient position of subservience.

I have also tried to show that openness does not create intelligence. Rather, it establishes the conditions in which the growth of intelligence is possible. The "design features" of an open organism assume that it will be in active commerce with the environment. Play, exploration, curiosity—those familiar symptoms of youth in so many mammals—are some of the many ways in which the organism educates itself. It is perhaps not too fanciful to say that the "open" organism feeds on information. Deprivation means that some of these activities are curtailed and in this case openness creates a definite risk. If deprivation is severe enough it can lead to radical and permanent impairment of information processing systems. Although even these extreme forms of deprivation continue to be a problem to man, they are less common, more easily remedied, and certainly less difficult to appraise, than those more subtle forms of deprivation that for all practical purposes leave the organism functionally intact, but unprepared to move on to the higher-order achievements of which it is potentially capable.

A biological perspective has helped us to understand the diverse sources of these achievements, to recognize the cumulative nature of intellectual growth, and to appreciate how the higher levels of intellectual functioning are critically dependent upon the prior development and the integrity of the levels that lie beneath them. It cannot help us to fulfill the human potential for achievement, nor to establish its limits. Here, at least, I think we must agree with Pope, that the proper study of mankind, indeed, is man.

ACKNOWLEDGMENT

Preparation of this chapter was assisted by National Institutes of Health grants FR00164-08 and HD03915.

REFERENCES

Berlyne, D. E. Curiosity and exploration. *Science,* 1966, **153,** 25-33.
Birch, H. G. The relation of previous experience to insightful problem solving. *Journal Comparative Psychology,* 1945, **38,** 367-383.
Bjorkman, M. Predictive behavior. *Scandinavian Journal of Psychology,* 1966, 7, 43-57.
Brunswik, E. Representative design and probabilistic theory in a functional psychology. *Psychological Review,* 1955, **62,** 193-215.
Butler, R. A. Acquired drives and the curiosity-investigative motives. In R. H. Waters, D. A. Rethlingshafer, & W. E. Caldwell (Eds.), *Principles of comparative psychology.* New York: McGraw-Hill, 1960.
Cross, H. A., & Harlow, H. F. Prolonged and progressive effects of partial isolation on the behavior of macaque monkeys. *Journal of Experimental Research in Personality,* 1965, 1, 39-49.
Davenport, R. K., & Rogers, C. M. Intellectual performance of differentially reared chimpanzees: I. Delayed response. *American Journal of Mental Deficiency,* 1968, **72,** 674-680.
Davenport, R. K., Rogers, C. M., & Menzel, E. W. Intellectual performance of differentially reared chimpanzees: II. Discrimination-learning set. *American Journal of Mental Deficiency,* 1969, **73,** 963-969.
Foley, J. P. Experimental investigation of the effect of prolonged inversion of the visual field in the rhesus monkey. *Journal of Genetic Psychology,* 1940, **56,** 21-51.
Forgays, D. G., & Forgays, J. W. The nature of the effect of free-environmental experience in the rat. *Journal of Comparative Physiological Psychology,* 1952, **45,** 322-328.
Forgus, R. H. The effect of early perceptual learning on the behavioral organization of adult rats. *Journal of Comparative Physiological Psychology,* 1954, **47,** 331-336.
Fuller, J. L. Experiential deprivation and later behavior. *Science,* 1967, **158,** 1645-1652.
Gallup, G. G., Jr. Chimpanzees: Self-recognition. *Science,* 1970, **167,** 86-87.
Guilford, J. P. Intelligence has three facets. *Science,* 1968, **160,** 615-620.
Harlow, H. F. The formation of learning sets. *Psychological Review,* 1949, **56,** 51-65.
Harlow, H. F., & Zimmermann, R. R. The development of affectional responses in infant monkeys. *Amer. Phil. Soc.,* 1958, **5,** 501-509.
Hayes, K. J. Genes, drives, and intellect. *Psychological Reports,* 1962, **10,** 299-342.
Held, R. Plasticity in sensory-motor systems. *Sci. Amer.,* 1965, **213,** 84-94.

Held, R., & Bauer, J. A., Jr. Visually guided reaching in infant monkeys after restricted rearing. *Science,* 1967, **155,** 718-720.

Held, R., & Hein, A. Movement-produced stimulation in the development of visually guided behavior. *Journal of Comparative Physiological Psychology,* 1963, **56,** 872-876.

Hunt, J. McV. *Intelligence and experience.* New York: Ronald Press, 1961.

Hymovitch, B. F. The effects of experimental variations on problem solving in the rat. *Journal of Comparative Physiological Psychology,* 1952, **45,** 313-321.

Kaess, W., & Kaess, F. Perception of apparent motion in the common toad. *Science,* 1960, **132,** 953.

Kuttner, R. An hypothesis on the evolution of intelligence. *Psychological Reports,* 1960, **6,** 283-289.

Lashley, K. S. Persistent problems in the evolution of mind. *Quart. Rev. Biol.,* 1949, **24,** 28-42.

Lorenz, K., & Tinbergen, N. Taxis and instinctive action in the egg-retrieving behavior of the greylag goose. In C. H. Schiller (Ed.), *Instinctive behavior.* New York: International Universities Press, 1957.

Maier, N. R. F. & Schneirla, T. C. *Principles of animal psychology.* New York: McGraw-Hill, 1935.

Marler, P., & Hamilton, W. J., III. *Mechanisms of animal behavior.* New York: Wiley, 1966.

Mason, W. A. The effects of social restriction on the behavior of rhesus monkeys: I. Free social behavior. *Journal of Comparative Physiological Psychology,* 1960, **53,** 582-589.

Mason, W. A., & Green, P. H. The effects of social restriction on the behavior of rhesus monkeys: IV. Responses to a novel environment and to an alien species. *Journal of Comparative Physiological Psychology,* 1962, **55,** 363-368.

Mason, W. A., & Sponholz, R. R. Behavior of rhesus monkeys raised in isolation. *Journal of Psychiatric Research,* 1963, **1,** 299-306.

Melzack, R. Effects of early experience on behavior: Experimental and conceptual considerations. In P. H. Hoch & J. Zubin (Eds.), *Psychopathology of perception.* New York: Grune & Stratton, 1965.

Melzack, R. Early experience: A neuropsychological approach to heredity-environment interactions. In G. Newton & S. Levine (Eds.), *Early experience and behavior.* Springfield, Ill.: Thomas, 1968.

Melzack, R., & Burns, S. K. Neurophysiological effects of early sensory restriction. *Experimental Neurology,* 1965, **13,** 163-175.

Menzel, E. W., Davenport, R. K., & Rogers, C. M. The development of tool using in wild-born and restriction-reared chimpanzees. *Folia Primatol.,* 1970, **12,** 273-283.

Noble, G. K. *The biology of the amphibia.* New York: McGraw-Hill, 1931.

Riesen, A. H. Excessive arousal effects of stimulation after early sensory deprivation. In P. Solomon, P. E. Kubzansky, P. H. Leiderman, J. H. Mendelson, R. Trumbull, & D. Wexler (Eds.), *Sensory deprivation.* Cambridge, Mass.: Harvard University Press, 1961.

Riesen, A. H. Sensory deprivation. In E. Stellar & J. Spraque (Eds.), *Progress in physiological psychology.* New York: Academic Press, 1966.

Rumbaugh, D. M. Maternal care in relation to infant behavior in the squirrel monkey. *Psychological Reports,* 1965, **16,** 171-176.

Sackett, G. P. Some persistent effects of different rearing conditions of preadult social behavior of monkeys. *Journal of Comparative Physiological Psychology,* 1967, **64,** 363-365.

Sperry, R. W. Mechanisms of neural maturation. In S. S. Stevens (Ed.), *Handbook of experimental psychology.* New York: Wiley, 1951.

Stenhouse D. A general theory for the evolution of intelligent behavior. *Nature, London,* 1965, **208,** 815.

Stratton, G. M. Vision without inversion of the retinal image. *Psychological Review,* 1897, **4,** 341-360.

Teuber, H. Lacunae and research approaches to them. I. In F. L. Darley (Ed.), *Brain mechanisms underlying speech and language.* New York: Grune & Stratton, 1967.

Thompson, W. R., & Heron, W. The effects of restricting early experience on the problem-solving capacity of dogs. *Canadian Journal of Psychology,* 1954, **8,** 17-31.

Thorpe, W. H. *Learning and instinct in animals.* Cambridge, Mass.: Harvard University Press, 1956.

Tinbergen, N. The hierarchical organization of nervous mechanisms underlying instinctive behavior. *Symposia of the Society for Experimental Biology,* 1950, **4,** 305-312.

von Foerster, H. From stimulus to symbol: The economy of biological computation. In W. Buckley (Ed.), *Modern systems research for the behavioral scientist.* Chicago: Aldine, 1968.

Warren, J. M. The comparative psychology of learning. *Annual Review of Psychology,* 1965, **16,** 95-118.

Welker, W. I. An analysis of exploratory and play behavior in animals. In D. W. Fiske & S. R. Maddi (Eds.), *Functions of varied experience.* Homewood, Ill.: Dorsey Press, 1961.

Wilson, M., Warren, J. M., & Abbott, L. Infantile stimulation, activity, and learning by cats. *Child Development,* 1965, **36,** 843-853.

Chapter 4

Effects of Group Rearing Conditions during the Preschool Years of Life[1] Hanŭs Papoušek

One may think of the child, the family, and society as making up the three sides of a triangle. The interactions and pressures among these sides cause a marked increase in tension on all components. Children cry for help, parents believe that governments could do more, and governments ask scientists to recommend the best ways. One answer is to pay more attention to the

[1]*Editor's note.* Dr. Papoušek was unable to leave Czechoslovakia to come to the AAAS meeting in Boston to present his paper. By the time he found out that he would not be able to come, it was too late for him to prepare a paper to send over to be read. Fortunately, I had visited with Papoušek in Prague and England in 1967, and I had seen him in this country while he was a visiting professor at Harvard in 1968. During these visits I had collected various material from him and I put this material together into a short presentation which I read at the Symposium as his contribution. Because Papoušek's material was in rough draft form, he did not have full references for his citations. In some instances, I have been able to obtain the appropriate citation; in other instances I have updated the references when I was aware that he wanted to make a general citation or when conference proceedings were ultimately published (e.g., we were together at a conference in London in 1967; these papers were published in 1969).

early preschool development of children. There are many different ways of improving preschool education, but all of these methods usually bring the child into a group of other children, and many people would like to know what effects the group rearing conditions may have upon the child's development. At this point the tensions in the triangle are transferred to the scientist, since the discrepancy between the number of problems connected with group rearing and the scarcity of studies concerned with solving those problems is embarrassing.

Yet, in many countries there are highly developed and organized systems of preschool facilities, including ones concerned with the care of infants. In many instances the trial-and-error method of looking for new ways of improving rearing conditions has been preferred. One major purpose of these systems is to give women the same rights to public activities as men have, thus profiting from the reserve intellectual and manual power of women (e.g., in war times). In Socialist countries such systems are organized, financed, and supervised by the state. In the USSR this has been done for 52 years, but even there mainly on an empirical base.

I will concentrate only upon the most disputable part of the problem, i.e., the day-care centers, which I personally studied in the USSR, England, Sweden, and Czechoslovakia. I also became familiar with these as a coorganizer of the First International Symposium on Day Centers in Prague in 1966. In Socialist countries the day-care centers are concerned only with the population from 0 to 3 years, and assistance is provided by the health authorities; whereas the care for older preschool children is provided by school authorities in kindergartens.

According to the International Labor Office Report of 1964, there are three main trends which are creating new needs for day-care centers: (1) constantly increasing number of women participating in gainful economic activities; (2) a progressive shift of economically active women from agriculture to industry, commerce, or services; and (3) far-reaching political and cultural changes in the status of women. In the United States women now make up a third of the total work force; in the USSR more than half; in Czechoslovakia, 45%; and in other East European countries, 40-50%. The number of mothers with dependent children among employed women is also increasing, even in the United States. In 1961 there were about 3 million mothers in the labor force with children of preschool age.

The present and future needs for day-care centers are not easy to determine. In 1966 the day centers could care for 26% of the population under 3 in the Soviet Ukraine, for 10% in Czecho-slovakia, and 17% in East Germany; but the estimated need was 50% in the Ukraine, 18% in Czechoslovakia, and 30% in East Germany. The number of places in day-care centers is reported to be insufficient in most European countries. To a certain degree the need for centers depends on the economic situation in the family, but not entirely. For example, starting in 1967 Hungarian mothers could be paid by the state for taking care of their children under 2½, but only a part of them preferred this advantage to the chance of using the help of day-care centers and continuing their economic activity.

Well furnished and equipped centers with sufficient staff are rather expensive, and the expenses are only partly covered by parents' contributions (21% of total expenses in Czechoslovakia, for instance). The expenses per child reimbursed by the state represent a substantial part of the mother's mean earning (40-50%). If there were no advantages to the day centers, it would be more economical to give mothers with two children paid maternal leaves rather than two places in day-care centers.

But let us now consider the potential advantages of day-care centers under *ideal* conditions, from the point of view of child rearing.

(1) Well-trained staff in sufficient numbers can help to raise the level of educational care above the average level usually found in families. In our country, 15 infants are cared for by one fully-trained nurse (2 years of training in general nursing and 2 in pediatric nursing) and one auxilliary nurse with short-term training. They are supervised by the center director and by a

pediatrician. Central governmental authorities provide them with detailed instructions and programs for all age groups, including the first year of life.

(2) The presence of group mates of similar age may positively influence the development of social behavior and of speech in every individual.

(3) Regular contact between parents and personnel may facilitate the transfer of important educational principles to families.

(4) Other proper conditions positively influencing the development of children may be established more easily than in homes, such as adequate space for play and outdoor activities, outdoor naps, selection and production of toys in agreement with pedagogic and hygienic principles, adequate nutrition, physical exercise, and inoculation and other preventative medical measures.

The actual effects of these potential advantages are determined by qualities of the personnel and economic factors, and any failure in these factors can turn the potential advantages into dangerous risks. Some of these risks are as follows:

(1) A lack of training or insufficient training of the staff can result in impersonal, cold, routine care, in poor emotional contact between children and adults and in accumulating conflict situations. Authoritarian central supervision of the centers tends to stress a normative approach to children, to neglect individual demands of children, and to support conformity. One problem, difficult to overcome, is the absence of men in day centers.

(2) The contact with group mates not only stimulates but also tires the child, and this sometimes turns into a real stress. Therefore, regulation of the amount of time in a group is necessary, particularly in newly admitted children during the period of adaptation to the unknown environment. Under group conditions, it is also more difficult to respect individual differences in behavioral state cycles, in the rhythm of concentration and relaxation, and in the demands of close contact with adults.

(3) Age homogeneity of the groups represents an epidemiological risk, too, facilitating the spread of some infectious agents, such as adenovirus or Rous Sarcomavirus.

(4) Any tendency to take away the responsibility for child rearing from parents may result in an unfavorable decrease in parental responsibility and in maternal or paternal deprivation. In particular, inexperienced young parents tend to shed their educational responsibility, either because of their fears concerning the difficulties of child rearing or because of the presence of a nearby day-care center. Such parents underestimate their irreplaceable role in child rearing and do not pay sufficient educational attention to their children at home.

(5) Day-care centers provide more play and useful activities, but, on the other hand, they detach the child from everyday contact with a broader environment, adult human activities in different situations, and nature. The child's view of these things is mostly mediated, narrowed, and flattened, and this may slow down the development of his speech and cognition.

It is evident that the problems of group rearing are complicated ones and difficult to solve in simple experimental tests. In fact, their list is a list of topics for future research.

In connection with group rearing, the question of environmental enrichment is frequently raised. The remarkable effects of small amounts of extra handling on the subsequent development of laboratory-reared animals (Denenberg, 1969; Levine, 1962) encouraged similar attempts in institutionalized human infants (White & Castle, 1964; White & Held, 1966). But contemporary textbooks on child rearing in day-care centers recommend so much handling, training, and stimulation that the value of any further quantitative increase seems questionable. Instead, more attention should be paid to the quality of stimulation.

Starting during the first few months of life, the human infant is able to respond to external stimulation with unconditioned responses (Papoušek, 1969). Equally important, he is also able to detect structure in the environmental stimulation, to perceive the relationship between different kinds of stimulation, and to adapt the patterns of his behavior to that structure (Bruner, 1969; Papoušek, 1969). According to contemporary neurophysiological findings (Miller, Galanter, & Pribram, 1960), the infant builds up neuronal models or plans of stimulation patterns and constantly compares his actual informational input with those plans; and he also compares the actual outcome of his responses with outcomes expected on the basis of his plans. The congruency or incongruency resulting from such comparisons elicit different consequences. With incongruency, the uncertainty in the system of behavioral regulation increases, and the mechanisms of information input and information processing are mobilized in order to reduce uncertainty. If this fails, the regulatory system inhibits the information input and processing and tries to get back to the preceding state of lower uncertainty. Congruency, on the contrary, reinforces temporary connections between stimuli and responses, reduces uncertainty in the regulatory system, and is accompanied by pleasant emotional experience.

The fundamental regulation plans built up in the first year of life represent an obviously important base for further mental development, but they require special conditions. The infant needs many trials to learn the structural relations among environmental stimuli, and he can communicate only through those channels that are already operative (proprioceptors, tactile receptors, smell, taste, and, later on, telereceptors). This is true in his communication with adults as well. Once the infant in regular contact with an adult learns the signal values of his behavior, this adult becomes an important mediator between the infant and his complicated and changing environment. The adult helps him to analyze information and to find the optimal responses.

In good rearing conditions the key learning situations are repeated frequently and regularly enough for the infant to understand their structural relations, and they also are repeated in different modifications and connections so that later the child learns the general validity of these relations and is able to develop a general abstraction. Koltsova clearly demonstrated, in her experiments on the development of speech, that a newly acquired word can become an abstract signal only after the child has had enough opportunity to become acquainted with the content of that word through all sensory channels and in different connections.

We hold that the child–mother relation is highly important, not only because of its emotional and social aspects, but above all, because of its role in the cognitive development of the child. And we assume, too, that a well-established relation with one adult person facilitates the establishment of relations with other adults and aids in the gradual social adjustment in the child. From this point of view, parents can never be successfully substituted in day-care centers, and the parents should be encouraged to reduce the length of the child's stay in a center to the necessary minimum.

The result of the various studies reporting unfavorable consequences of early maternal deprivation (Bowlby, 1951; Goldfarb, 1955; Spitz, 1945) and recently also of paternal deprivation was to intensify the tendency to avoid institutional care for children, to shorten the stay of infants in day centers, to stop building up centers with permanent day and night service, and to refuse admissions of infants into day centers before the sixth month of age. Thus, in Czechoslovakia the laws concerning adopting children without adequate family care were revised, residential infant homes were replaced with foster homes, and maternal paid leave was extended to 6 months after delivery.

The tendency to postpone admittance to the day centers is at variance with the findings that separation from families and adaptation to new environments is easier in infants below 6 months than in infants between 6 and 18 months. Difficult adaptation causing loss in weight, disturbed sleep, and disturbed behavior can be avoided if the infant only spends short times in the center together with his mother during the first days or weeks, as is common in England.

In comparison with children brought up at home, the children in day-care centers usually show delays in the development of speech, oculomotor coordination, and social behavior, although in somatic and motor development they are equal or slightly better than children in families. Sheynbergas and Kukinene reported that in a good institution infants admitted before the fifth month of life crawled and walked sooner than infants admitted from their homes at later ages, but they were slower in speech development. The differences are believed to prove that the positive influence of group rearing in infants is overshadowed by the negative consequences of parental deprivation.

It is very difficult, though, to differentiate the effects of insufficient rearing conditions from the effects of increased morbidity in day-care centers, usually reported to be twice as high as in families. In residential centers, the morbidity is again twice as high as in day centers. According to Pavlásková, the morbidity is significantly higher in the age group from 9 to 18 months and during the first 6 weeks of stay in centers, so that it might be connected with difficult separation and adaptation, but it is not possible to say, definitely, which of them is primary.

I have attempted to review briefly the problems and effects of group rearing in day-care centers. Unfortunately, one has to rely more upon practical and clinical experiences than on theoretical issues and experimental verification, but this only reflects the actual state of knowledge of such an important process as that of bringing up our future generations. This state seems to be typical of the present situation of mankind whose courage to experiment with atomic fission is greater than the courage to study their own minds.

REFERENCES

Bowlby, J.   Maternal care and mental health. *World Health Organization Monograph,* 1951, No. 2.

Bruner, J. Processes of growth in infancy. In J. A. Ambrose (Ed.), *Stimulation in early infancy.* New York: Academic Press, 1969.

Denenberg, V. H. The effects of early experience. In E. S. E. Hafez (Ed.), *The behaviour of domestic animals.* London: Baillière, 1969. pp. 95-130.

Goldfarb, W. Emotional and intellectual consequences of psychological deprivation in infancy: A revaluation. In P. H. Hoch & J. Zubin (Eds.),

Psychopathology of childhood. New York: Grune & Stratton, 1955. pp. 105-119.

Levine, S. The psychophysiological effects of infantile stimulation. In E. L. Bliss (Ed.), *Roots of behavior.* New York: Harper, 1962. pp. 246-253.

Miller, G. A., Galanter, E., & Pribram, K. H. *Plans and the structure of behavior.* New York: Holt, 1960.

Papoušek, H. The functions of conditioning stimulation in human neonates and infants. In J. A. Ambrose (Ed.), *Stimulation in early infancy.* New York: Academic Press, 1969.

Spitz, R. A. Hospitalism. An inquiry into the genesis of psychiatric conditions in early childhood. *Psychoanalytic Studies of the Child,* 1945, **1**, 53-74.

White, B. L., & Castle, P. W. Visual exploratory behavior following postnatal handling of human infants. *Perceptual and Motor Skills,* 1964, **18**,497-502.

White, B. L. & Held, R. Plasticity of sensorimotor development in the human infant. In J. F. Rosenblith & W. Allinsmith (Eds.), *Readings in child development and educational psychology.* (2nd ed.) Boston: Allyn & Bacon, 1966.

Chapter 5

Need
for Early
and Continuing
Education | *Earl S. Schaefer*

The growing evidence that early experience influences later academic achievement has motivated the development of a number of experimental nursery school programs. More recently, infant education programs have been designed to prevent the low levels of intellectual functioning that are found in disadvantaged children as early as 3 years of age. The accumulating data on the short-term and long-term effects of early education programs as well as data from cross-sectional and longitudinal studies of intellectual development prompted this analysis of the need for early and continuing education. Research data on intellectual development and academic achievement also suggested the need for reevaluation of current implicit answers to the questions: "By whom, where, when, how, and in what characteristics should the child be educated?"

A COMPREHENSIVE DEFINITION OF EDUCATION

A reevaluation of these basic questions about the process of education may lead to expansion of the current restricted meaning of "education." A comprehensive definition of education includes "the act or process of rearing or bringing up ..." and "the process of providing with knowledge, skill, competence

or usually desirable qualities of behavior and character . . ."
(Webster's *Third New International Dictionary of the English
Language,* Unabridged, G. and C. Merriam Company, Springfield,
Massachusetts, 1965.) However, both popular and professional
discussions of education usually assume a more restricted
meaning, i.e., the activities of professional educators teaching the
traditional academic subjects to school-age children in the
schools, which is a description of formal or academic education.

An analysis of the more comprehensive definition of education suggests that academic education is only one component of
the total education system. In recognition of the current focus on
academic education, other components might be labeled *pre-
academic education* for education prior to school entrance,
paraacademic education for education by extraacademic institutions during the school years, and *postacademic education* for
continuing education after the school years. Recognition of the
importance of these extraacademic components of education may
be necessary in order to design an education system that would
be more successful in promoting the adjustment and competence
of disadvantaged social groups.

NEED FOR A DISCIPLINE OF UR-EDUCATION

A possible response to recognition of the importance of early
experience and of the need for early and continued education
might be the extension of academic education to earlier as well as
subsequent ages. An attempt to apply the assumptions and
methods of academic education to early education might accom-
pany this temporal extension of academic education. An alternative strategy might be to use research on existing methods of pre-
and paraacademic education as a basis for the development of
early education. The educational needs of young children
probably differ greatly from those of children who are ready to
participate in academic education. The development of a new
discipline of *Ur-education,* a suggested label for the most

primitive—earliest and most basic—education of the child, may be required in order to develop more effective approaches to early education. Although academic education would contribute to this development, the behavioral sciences, particularly the growth sciences, might provide a scientific basis for that discipline. Since parents have had the primary responsibility for early education, studies of parent-child relationships may be the best source of information for the development of Ur-education.

As an example of how research on parent-child relationships might contribute to the development of Ur-education, I will briefly outline a four-stage model for the early education of the child. The model was suggested by the accumulating evidence of the importance of parental loving acceptance as opposed to hostile rejection for the social, emotional, and cognitive development of the child. The four stages that are logically, if not temporally, differentiable suggest possible approaches to improving the early education of the child. The first stage is the development by the parent of a positive attachment to the child.

(Stage 1)

In the second stage, the positive involvement of the parent elicits from the child the development of a positive relationship with the parent.

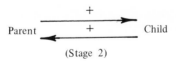

(Stage 2)

In the third stage, the parent and child together engage in an activity or explore an object. In the context of this experience,

through both verbal and nonverbal behavior, the parent educates
the child.

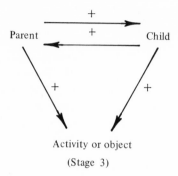

Activity or object

(Stage 3)

The fourth stage suggests that from this early experience with the
parent the child has acquired the interests, the motivation, and
the skills that allow him to function effectively as an autonomous
student.

Child ——————+——————▶ Activity or object

(Stage 4)

Achievement of these early developmental stages may be a
necessary basis for successful participation in academic education.

EMERGENCE OF DIFFERENCES IN MENTAL
TEST SCORES AMONG SOCIAL GROUPS

The need for early education is suggested by studies that find
that schools typically do not increase the low levels of intellectual
functioning that disadvantaged children acquire prior to school

entrance. Data from a sample of black children from the southeastern states revealed a low mean IQ on the Stanford-Binet at school entrance that did not change during the school years (Kennedy, 1969; Kennedy, Van De Riet, & White, 1963; Schaefer, 1965b). In contrast to the relatively stable Stanford-Binet scores of that group, Coleman (1966) reports a consistent decline in the verbal ability of blacks during the school years. When data were examined by regions, large declines were found in the South and Southwest outside metropolitan areas and little or no decline in Northeast, Midwest, and West metropolitan areas. Although these data suggest that different areas support different rates of intellectual growth during the school years, Coleman found that in none of the regions did the differences between whites and blacks decrease during the school years. These findings suggest a need to prevent the low levels of functioning that develop prior to school entrance as well as to increase the rate of intellectual development during the school years.

Normative data for the Stanford-Binet suggest that differences between social groups in mean intelligence test scores may be established prior to 3 years of age. Differences among mean IQ scores of children from different occupational groups were as large for children between 2 and 5½ years as they were for subsequent age groups (Terman, 1937). Both Van Alstyne (1929) and Hindley (1965) found substantial relationships between socioeconomic status and mental test scores at 3 years of age. Schaefer (1969) found a mean Bayley Infant Mental test IQ of 90 at 21 months that remained at that level through 4 years of age for a control group of urban black male infants from low socioeconomic status families.

In contrast to these findings, several studies have found no clear evidence of IQ differences between social groups through 18 months of age. Bayley (1965) found little difference in mean mental test scores by socioeconomic status or ethnic group through 15 months. Hindley (1965) found no meaningful difference by socioeconomic status at 18 months, although he found clear differences between socioeconomic groups at 3 years.

Francis-Williams and Yule (1967) confirmed Bayley's finding of little relationship between socioeconomic status and Bayley Infant Mental Test scores between 1 and 15 months. Schaefer (1969) also found that disadvantaged black male infants did not have low Bayley scores at 14 months.

The consistent finding of no relationship between socio-economic status and IQ scores prior to 15 months and of significant correlations by 3 years might be related to variations in the functions measured at different ages. Hofstaetter's (1954) factor analysis of Bayley's (1949) intercorrelations of mental test scores between birth and 18 years revealed three different factors that contributed to mental test scores at different ages during the first 6 years of life. Cronbach (1967) questioned whether factor analysis could identify unique factors for specific age periods but did not question the finding that different factors are found for different ages.

LANGUAGE DEVELOPMENT
AND INTELLECTUAL DEVELOPMENT

The appearance of differences in mean mental test scores of different social groups is probably related to changes in the content of mental tests from sensory motor items to language items. The Bayley Scales of Infant Mental Development (1969) include few language-skill items prior to 18 months of age and a large number of such items after 24 months. Additional support for this interpretation is given by evidence of rapid language development during the second year of life (McCarthy, 1954).

A number of studies suggest the importance of early language development for the future intellectual development of the child. Bradway (1945) found that, of several components derived from the Stanford-Binet, verbal scores during the early years yielded better predictions of intelligence than nonverbal or memory scores. Bayley (1966) has also reported that a factor of verbal knowledge yields higher predictions of future intelligence than other factors isolated from tests between 2 and 6 years of age.

The effectiveness of early language skills in predicting later intellectual level may be attributed to the high relationships between standard mental tests and verbal comprehension as measured by vocabulary items. Templin (1958) found in her study of language development of children between 3 and 8 years of age that "Only the relationship between intelligence and vocabulary was substantial and was maintained throughout the age span of three to eight." Miner (1957), in a review of studies that correlated vocabulary scores with total scores on the Stanford-Binet' and Wechsler-Bellevue, found that vocabulary typically correlates above .80 with total scores. Correlations of vocabulary with total score are usually as great as the correlations of the two major mental tests with one another. A number of studies have shown substantial relationships between socio-economic status and language skills, particularly verbal comprehension. Templin (1958) found that most language measures were related to socioeconomic status. A number, including vocabulary of recognition at school ages, were more related to socioeconomic status than were intelligence test scores. In a study by Sitkei and Myers (1969) of 100 4-year-old children, equally divided into low and middle socioeconomic status and white and black groups, six interpretable factors were extracted from intercorrelations of 22 tests. Only a factor of verbal comprehension showed significant differences by socioeconomic status and by ethnic groups.

A focus upon early verbal development is also supported by studies of the relationship between vocabulary and academic success. Werner, Simonian, and Smith (1967) reported that the verbal comprehension subtest of the Thurstone Primary Mental Abilities is the best single predictor of reading achievement. Relatively little improvement in prediction was found for a multiple correlation including other measures. Miner (1957) concluded from his review of the literature that vocabulary is the best single predictor of both academic and occupational achievement.

The evidence of the coincidence of the emergence of early language skills with the emergence of mental test differences between social groups, of the relationship of early language measures with later intelligence, and of the relationship of verbal skills to socioeconomic status, ethnic group, IQ scores, reading achievement, and academic and occupational success, supports a conclusion that the education of the child should begin prior to or at the beginning of the period of early language development. Since it is reasonable to assume that the development of relationships, interests, motivation, and other characteristics during the first year of life may influence subsequent verbal development, the course that would be most likely to support the child's optimal development would be to assume that age-appropriate education, in the more universal sense, should begin at birth.

Research findings that early sensory-motor and nonverbal skills have little relationship to later intellectual functioning would not support a hypothesis that accelerating the development of those skills will influence later intelligence test scores. These research data also suggest the need for caution in implicitly adopting a *post hoc ergo propter hoc* interpretation of Piaget's early developmental stages.

CONTINUING INFLUENCE OF ENVIRONMENT

An interpretation of the data on early verbal and intellectual development as supporting the need for early education assumes that differences in early experience produce differences in intellectual development. Only a few relevant studies from the extensive literature on the roles of heredity and environment in intellectual development that would support that assumption will be reviewed here. The discussion will focus upon evidence that the rate of intellectual development is related to the quality of the environment and that changes in the environment are related to changes in the rate of intellectual development. Thus both increases in mental test scores with increases in stimulation and decreases in test scores after termination of educational intervention would support the hypothesis that experience influences intellectual development.

In a pioneering study, Skeels and Dye (1939) found large IQ gains for orphanage infants considered to be seriously retarded who were transferred to a ward of an institution for mentally retarded women, while the contrast group in the orphanage showed decrements in IQ. After the experimental children had achieved higher mental test scores, 11 of the 13 were placed in adoptive homes. A follow-up at maturity found major differences in the life histories of the two groups (Skeels, 1966). The different histories of the two experimental subjects who were not adopted would support a hypothesis that the continuing support for intellectual growth provided by the adoptive homes, as well as the continued residence of the control group in a limited environment, might be as important as the dramatic effects of the early intervention in producing the differences between groups found at maturity.

The hypothesis that Skeels' and Dye's children would have regressed in mean IQ scores if they had been returned to the orphanage environment is supported by follow-up studies of successful early education projects. Gray and Klaus (1969) have reported the Stanford-Binet scores of their early training project children after termination of their program of summer school and home visits that had produced highly significant IQ differences between experimental and control group children. Although the mean IQ scores of their experimental groups increased consistently during the period of intervention, their mean IQ scores had declined approximately 10 points three years after the intervention ended. Gray and Klaus concluded that "the evidence on human performance is overwhelming in indicating that such performance results from the continual interaction of the organism with its environment."

Caldwell and Smith (1968) also reported large IQ gains from

participation in a university day-care program that included a heavy focus upon intellectual stimulation. Retesting a year after the children had left the program revealed that "Their functioning level had shown a rather sharp drop from the point at which they functioned just prior to leaving the program, but they still scored slightly higher than a group of matched controls . . ."

Schaefer (1969) has also reported that disadvantaged infants who were provided child-centered home tutoring between 15 and 36 months showed accelerated intellectual growth during the tutoring period, but a decrement in mean Stanford-Binet IQ from 106 to 100 a year after termination of tutoring. Although the tutored group's mean IQ score had dropped, their mean Stanford-Binet IQ was still 10 points above that of the control group.

Studies by Klineberg (1935) and Lee (1957) of blacks who moved from the South to northern urban centers indicate that IQ scores can increase during the school years. In a study of Southern - born black children who entered the Philadelphia schools, Lee (1957) found small IQ gains for those who entered the fifth and sixth grades and larger IQ gains for those who entered the first grade. Mean IQ scores apparently continued to increase over a 4- to 6-year period for groups entering at each grade level. On the sixth-grade mental test, the immigrant group who entered in the first grade approached the mean IQ level of the Philadelphia-born who did not attend kindergarten but lagged behind children who had attended kindergarten. Perhaps attendance at kindergarten was an index of family environment for that sample. Increases in IQ of the children might have been influenced by changes in the extraacademic environment as well as by changes in academic education.

The hypothesis that level of intellectual functioning can change dramatically at later ages with a major change in the person's environment receives strong support from longitudinal data on about 200 adolescent and adult patients who had been certified as feebleminded (Clarke & Clarke, 1959, 1960). These were all severely deprived defectives drawn either from adverse or exceptionally adverse backgrounds. After 6 years in an improved environment, 33% of the group from exceptionally adverse home environments showed increments of more than 20 IQ points, and a majority showed IQ gains of 10 points or more. IQ increments were greater in those who had suffered the most serious deprivation. These data would suggest that the stability of IQ of the individual is proportional to the stability of his environment and that significant increases in IQ can be produced by significant increases in the quality of the environment.

Evidence that significant changes in intellectual functioning can occur during the adult years was found by Bayley (1966) in her correlations between Wechsler-Bellevue IQ scores at 16 and those at 36 years. Although the correlation for males was .97, the correlation for females was only .69, a fact which reveals great changes in relative level of functioning for many women in the group. If women's roles in society are less consistently related to their intellectual functioning and provide less consistent opportunity to use intellectual abilities, greater fluctuation in intellectual functioning would result. Apart from an interpretation of the changes, the fact that intelligence test scores are not consistently stable during maturity would suggest that different environments may have different potentials for maintaining or fostering intellectual functioning of adults.

If the rate of intellectual growth is proportional to the rate of intellectual stimulation, then the amount of change in intellectual functioning that is produced by a move from one environment to another should be proportional to the extent of difference between the two environments. Clarke and Clarke (1959) report larger gains in IQ during maturity for feebleminded adults who had been reared in exceptionally adverse home environments than for those who had been reared in less adverse environments. They suggest that the amount of recovery can be taken as a minimal estimate of the amount of retardation related to early deprivation. From their studies of changes in IQ during maturity, they conclude that the most adverse social conditions retard intellectual development at least an average of 16 points, and that less severe deprivation can retard mental development by an average of 10 points. Their data on increases in intellectual functioning after leaving adverse home environments suggest that a major change in the environment can produce a major change in intellectual functioning even during maturity.

Coleman's (1966, p. 523) analysis of the apparent effects of Head Start upon test scores also suggests that supplementary or compensatory education programs may have their greatest effects upon the most disadvantaged children. He states,

> Controlling for race, region, kindergarten attendance, and various measures of socioeconomic status, it would appear that scores for participants were consistently higher than scores for nonparticipants from the same schools for pupils from the poorest families: Negroes of low SES, particularly those in rural areas. For Negroes from higher socioeconomic-status, and whites, effects of Head Start participation could not be detected from ability test scores in any concrete patterns. Verbal ability—as measured by the tests—was affected to a greater degree than nonverbal ability where effects of Head Start were found.

This analysis does not control for possible higher motivation among deprived families that elect to participate in Head Start.

Proponents of early education programs frequently cite Bloom's (1964) conclusion, derived from longitudinal data on intellectual development, that "in terms of intelligence measured at age 17, at least 20% is developed by age 1, 50% by about age 4, 80% by about age 8 and 92% by age 13." From the perspective that the environment may have an impact upon intellectual development at every period of development, the subjects that were used, mostly children reared in their own homes from birth to maturity, do not provide an adequate empirical basis for that conclusion. Perhaps a child's later intelligence is predictable because a child has a stable environment that fosters a stable rate of intellectual growth. If children at 4 years were randomly assigned to environments that varied in their stimulation of intellectual growth, later intelligence would probably be less predictable. This criticism of Bloom's often-quoted statement does not deny the importance of early development but would question the degree of irreversibility suggested by that statement.

Two contrasting hypotheses—(1) that the environment influences intellectual development at each period of development, or (2) that the child's mental level is irreversibly determined during the early years—would suggest different approaches to increasing intellectual development. The first hypothesis would support the development of family-centered programs that would attempt to foster changes in the child's continuing environment, while the second would suggest relatively intensive child-centered interventions during the early years.

PARENTAL INFLUENCE UPON MENTAL DEVELOPMENT

Studies of parent behavior and child development support a hypothesis that stable patterns of parental behavior influence the development of the child. Schaefer and Bayley (1960) found relatively high stability ($r = .68$) from infancy to adolescence for a dimension of maternal loving acceptance vs. hostile rejection. Broussard (1969) reported that mothers' negative perception of their infants at 1 month were significantly related to psychiatric judgments of the children's maladjustment at 4½ years of age.

Case studies and unpublished data suggest that mothers develop different relationships with different children. (A mother who accepted one child and rejected the other said at different times of the rejected child that he was ugly, was not cuddly, and looked like her husband.) Evidence that current stresses and the absence of social support influence maternal hostility, abuse, and neglect of the child suggests that attempts to alleviate the stress and increase the support of mothers at the time the initial mother-child relationship is developed might contribute to the development of maternal attachment.

Significant correlations between early ratings of maternal behavior and child's subsequent adjustment, task-oriented behavior, and mental test scores had been interpreted as revealing the cumulative effect of parent behavior upon child behavior (Schaefer & Bayley, 1963). Many studies suggest that the family environment provided by parents and parental behavior with the child may be a major factor in the early and continuing education of the child (Roff, 1950). Parents are major suppliers of the materials and experiences that contribute to the child's education and are the gatekeepers who control the child's access to society and society's access to the child.

The significance of parental behavior for intellectual development has been shown by a number of longitudinal and cross-sectional studies. An initial report on the Fels longitudinal study by Baldwin (1949) showed that a cluster of democratic behaviors of parents was related to increases in IQ. A recent analysis of Fels data by Kagan and Freeman (1963) and Kagan (1964) supported that initial finding for both sexes. A partial correlation which removed the relationship of maternal education to maternal behavior tended to reduce the size of the correlations of intelligence with a scale of Justification of Discipline although the correlations still remained significant, particularly for girls. Kagan and Freeman (1963) suggested that Justification of Discipline "not only verbally stimulates the child but also communicates a faith in his conceptual capacity."

Significant correlations were found between maternal behavior during the first 3 years of life and intellectual development of boys in the Berkeley Growth Study. Maternal ignoring, punitiveness, and perceiving the child as a burden were negatively correlated, and maternal equalitarianism was positively correlated with intellectual development of sons. Correlations of maternal behavior with intellectual development of daughters did not reveal significant relationships (Bayley & Schaefer, 1964). Similarly, maternal behavior showed more long-term correlation with social, emotional, and task-oriented behavior of sons than of daughters. In an effort to explain differences in correlations for males and females, Bayley and Schaefer (1964) proposed a hypothesis of "a genetic sex difference in resistance to or resilience in recovery from environmental influences."

In contrast to Bayley and Schaefer's finding, Hurley (1965, 1967) reported that measures related to parental acceptance vs. rejection, derived from inventories and interviews with parents of third-grade children, were more highly correlated with intelligence test scores of girls than of boys with significant correlations for both sexes. Hurley suggested that the discrepant findings for boys and girls in the Berkeley Growth Study might be attributed to instability of findings from small samples.

Hess, Shipman, Brophy, and Bear's (1969) study of urban preschool children provides strong support for a hypothesis that the cognitive environment significantly influences intellectual development of both boys and girls. Highly significant correlations were found between measures of cognitive development and academic achievement and measures of mother-child interaction derived from home visits and observations in an experimental setting. Among the measures correlating most highly with intelligence and academic achievement were ratings from home visits of the mothers' use of resources in the home to foster the child's cognitive development, and maternal support toward the child. Methods of maternal control, maternal language, and maternal teaching style, as well as maternal affection, were significantly correlated with the child's intellectual development and academic achievement. An early study by Van Alstyne (1929) revealed sizable correlations between parental practices such as reading to the child, contact with adults, and other family environment variables and the child's vocabulary at 3 years even after controlling by partial correlation the effects of maternal intelligence. Milner (1951) found that children from low socioeconomic status homes who earned low scores on a reading readiness test were read to less often, received less affection, were whipped more often, and shared mealtime conversations less often.

Analyses of longitudinal data by Moore (1968) provide further confirmation of the relationship of parent behavior to both intellectual development and the child's achievement in reading. Ratings of the toys, books, and experiences provided for the child, the quality and quantity of verbal stimulation of the child, and the quality of the parent-child relationship were made from home visits at the child's age of 2½ years. Correlations of these home-environment variables with the child's intelligence test scores at 3 and 8 years and reading achievement at 8 years were significant, even after partialling out socioeconomic status. The surprising predictive validity of home ratings made at 2½ years for the child's status at 8 years after controlling for SES provides strong confirmation of the hypothesis that parental behavior can influence the child's development and indirect evidence that patterns of parental behavior tend to remain stable through time.

A study of a group of disadvantaged black infants involved in a home tutoring program provides further confirmation of the finding of significant correlations between early maternal behavior and the child's intellectual development (Schaefer, 1969). Maternal behavior rating scales were completed from observations of mother-child interaction during tutoring sessions in the home. Significant correlations were found between a cluster of maternal behaviors that were labeled hostile uninvolvement, including low interest in the child's education, low verbal expressiveness with the child, low involvement with the child and hostile detachment, and the child's hostile maladjustment, poor task-oriented behavior, and low mental test scores at 3 years. A set of child-neglect variables including leaving the child without adult care, inadequate day care, irregular meals, inadequate clothing, sickness, accidents, and beatings were found to relate to maternal hostile uninvolvement and were also correlated with the child's development.

The different studies summarized above reveal that many children experience a combination of physical, social and emotional, and cultural deprivation. Although different types of deprivation can be differentiated, very large samples would be needed to determine their independent relationships to the child's development. This problem confronts investigators of the effects of malnutrition as well as those who are interested in the effects of social, emotional, and cultural variables. However, different hypotheses about the relative influence of the different types of deprivation might lead to very different programs designed to foster the optimal development of children. That loving involvement of the parent with the child would be related to better physical care and to greater cultural stimulation would appear to have face validity. In fact, reports by children of intellectual stimulation by the parent are highly correlated with reports of parental love and acceptance (Schaefer, 1965a).

Studies of relationships of parent behavior to the child's development provide consistent support for the emphasis on the quality of dyadic relationships in the proposed model for Ur-education. They also support the emphasis upon enriched experiences and parent-child communication about those experiences. The focus of this discussion has been upon intellectual development and academic achievement, with little attention to the social, emotional, and task-oriented behavior of the child. However, parental behaviors that tend to be related to intellectual development also tend to be related to adjustment, positive relationships with others, and task-oriented behaviors (Baldwin, 1949; Becker, 1964; Kagan & Moss, 1962; Schaefer & Bayley, 1963).

Recognition of the importance of parent behavior for the development of the child has led to the inclusion of training of parents in two successful preschool education programs (Klaus & Gray, 1968; Weikart, 1968). Preventing cognitive deficits by teaching parents more effective methods of educating their infants has been the major focus of infant-education projects developed by Gordon (1969) and Weikart (1969). Levenstein (1969) has reported success in promoting cognitive growth by stimulating verbal interaction of the mother with the child. Books and toys were conceptualized as "verbal interaction stimulus material." Their use was demonstrated to the mother in the home, after which the mother was encouraged to continue their use with the child. Mean IQ gains of 17 points were found in the experimental group after an average of 32 visits over a 7-month period during which a total of 28 books and toys were left in the home. If these results can be replicated, this clearly focused program is an effective and economical method for fostering early cognitive development.

SUMMARY AND IMPLICATIONS

The need for early education has been suggested by data on the emergence of differences between mean mental test scores of different social groups during the period of early verbal development: the second year of life. Evidence that language skills, particularly verbal comprehension, relate highly to intelligence test scores, to reading achievement, and to educational and occupational achievement was interpreted as suggesting that education should begin during or prior to the period of early, rapid language development.

Research findings that intellectual functioning is influenced by environmental stimulation during the school years, adolescence, and maturity were interpreted as evidence of the need for continued education to promote optimal intellectual development. Evidence that mean IQ scores increase during intensive intellectual stimulation and decrease after such stimulation is terminated was cited as supporting family-centered programs designed to increase adequacy of family education throughout the period of child development.

Research showing relationships of parent behavior and family environment to the child's development was reviewed. The apparent success of programs that have attempted to influence patterns of parent behavior with the child was noted.

If the evidence is convincing that intelligence and competence can be increased by early and continuing education, the development of a comprehensive system of education that would extend from birth through maturity is necessary. Academic education should be supplemented by the development of pre-, para-, and postacademic education in the family and community and by the mass media. Parents should be recognized as the most influential educators of their own children. A new discipline of Ur-education—early, basic education—should supplement the current system of academic education. Through research and development more refined models of early education and more effective methods and materials should be developed. However, current knowledge of the effect of early experience upon child development is sufficient to justify teaching skills in Ur-education to all persons—parents, future parents, educators, and child-care workers—who have, or will have, responsibility for the early education of children.

REFERENCES

Baldwin, A. L. The effect of home environment on nursery school behavior. *Child Development,* 1949, **20,**49-61.

Bayley, N. Consistency and variability in the growth of intelligence from birth to 18 years, *Journal of Genetic Psychology,* 1949, **75,** 165-196.

Bayley, N. Comparisons of mental and motor test scores for ages 1-15 months by sex, birth order, race, geographical location, and education of parents. *Child Development,* 1965, **36,**379-411.

Bayley, N. Learning in adulthood: the role of intelligence. In H. Klausmeier & C. Harris, (Eds.), *Analyses of concept learning.* New York: Academic Press, 1966.

Bayley, N. *Bayley scales of infant development.* New York: Psychological Corp., 1969.

Bayley, N., & Schaefer, E. S. Correlations of maternal and child behaviors with the development of mental abilities: data from the Berkeley growth study. *Monographs of the Society for Research in Child Development,* 1964, **29** (6, whole No. 97).

Becker, W. C., & Krug, R. S. A circumplex model for social behavior in children. *Child Development,* 1964, **35,**371-396.

Bloom, B. S. *Stability and change in human characteristics.* New York: Wiley, 1964.

Bradway, K. P. Predictive value of Stanford-Binet preschool items. *Journal of Educational Psychology,* 1945, **36,**1-16.

Broussard, E. R., & Hartner, S. S. Maternal perception of the neonate as related to development. Paper presented at the meeting of the American Psychiatric Association, Miami, May 1969.

Caldwell, B. M., & Smith, L. E. Day care for the very young: prime opportunity for primary prevention. Paper presented at the meeting of the American Public Health Association, Detroit, November 1968.

Clarke, A. D. B., & Clarke, A. M. Recovery from the effects of deprivation. *Acta Psychologica,* 1959, **16,** 137-144.

Clarke, A. D. B., & Clarke, A. M. Some recent advances in the study of early deprivation. *Journal of Child Psychology and Psychiatry,* 1960, **1,** 26-36.

Coleman, J. S. *Equality of educational opportunity.* Washington, D. C.: USGPO, 1966.

Cronbach, L. J. Year-to-year correlations of mental tests: a review of the Hofstaetter analysis. *Child Development,* 1967, **38,** 283-289.

Francis-Williams, J., & Yule, W. The Bayley infant scales of mental and motor development: An exploratory study with an English sample. *Developmental Medicine and Child Neurology,* 1967, **9,** 391-401.

Gordon, I. J. Stimulation via parent education. *Children,* 1969, **16,** 57-59.

Gray, S. W., & Klaus, R. A. The early training project: A seventh year report. John F. Kennedy Center for Research on Education and Human Development, George Peabody College for Teachers, 1969.

Hess, R. D., Shipman, V. C., Brophy, J. E. & Bear, R. M. The cognitive environments of urban pre-school children: Follow-up phase. Graduate School of Education, University of Chicago, 1969.

Hindley, C. B. Stability and change in abilities up to five years: Group trends, *Journal of Child Psychology and Psychiatry,* 1965, **6,** 85-99.

Hofstaetter, P. R. The changing composition of intelligence: A study in T-technique. *Journal of Genetic Psychology,* 1954, **85,** 159-164.

Hurley, J. R. Parental acceptance-rejection and children's intelligence. *Merrill-Palmer Quarterly,* 1965, **11,** 19-31.

Hurley, J. R. Parental malevolence and children's intelligence. *Journal of Consulting Psychology,* 1967, **31,** 199-204.

Kagan, J. Erratum. *Child Development,* 1964 **35,** 1397.

Kagan, J., & Freeman, M. Relation of childhood intelligence, maternal behaviors, and social class to behavior during adolescence. *Child Development,* 1963, **34,** 899-911.

Kagan, J., & Moss, H. A. *Birth to maturity: A study in psychological development.* New York: Wiley, 1962.

Kennedy, W. A. A follow-up normative study of Negro intelligence and achievement. *Monographs of the Society for Research in Child Development,* 1969, **34,** (2, whole No. 126).

Kennedy, W. A., Van De Riet, W., & White, J. C., Jr. A normative sample of intelligence and achievement of Negro elementary school children in the southeastern United States. *Monographs of the Society for Research in Child Development,* 1963, **28,** (6, whole No. 90).

Klaus, R. A., & Gray, S. W. The early training project for disadvantaged children: A report after five years. *Monographs of the Society for Research in Child Development,* 1968, **33,** (4, whole No. 120).

Klineberg, O. *Negro intelligence and selective migration.* New York: Columbia University Press, 1935.

Lee, E. S. Negro intelligence and selective migration: A Philadelphia test of the Klineberg hypothesis. *American Sociological Review,* 1957, **16,** 227-233.

Levenstein, P. Cognitive growth in preschoolers through stimulation of verbal interaction with mothers. Paper presented at the 46th annual meeting of the American Orthopsychiatric Association, New York, April 1969.

McCarthy, D. Language development in children. In L. Carmichael (Ed.), *Manual of child psychology.* (2nd ed.) New York: Wiley, 1954, pp. 492-630.

Milner, E. A study of the relationship between reading readiness in grade one school children and patterns of parent-child interaction. *Child Development,* 1951, **22,** 95-112.

Miner, J. B. *Intelligence in the United States.* New York: Springer, 1957.

Moore, T. Language and intelligence: A longitudinal study of the first 8 years. *Human Development,* 1968, **11,** 88-106.

Roff, M. Intra-family resemblances in personality characteristics. *Journal of Psychology,* 1950, **30,** 199-227.

Schaefer, E. S. A configurational analysis of children's reports of parent behavior. *Journal of Consulting Psychology,* 1965, **29,** 552-557. (a)

Schaefer, E. S. Does the sampling method produce the negative correlation of mean IQ with age reported by Kennedy, Van De Riet, and White. *Child Development,* 1965, **36,** 257-259. (b)

Schaefer, E. S. Home tutoring, maternal behavior and infant intellectual development. Paper presented at the meeting of the American Psychological Association, Washington, D. C., September 1969.

Schaefer, E. S., & Bayley, N. Consistency of maternal behavior from infancy to preadolescence. *Journal of Abnormal and Social Psychology,* 1960, **61,** 1-6.

Schaefer, E. S., & Bayley, N. Maternal behavior, child behavior, and their intercorrelations from infancy through adolescence. *Monographs of the Society for Research in Child Development,* 1963, **28,** (3, whole No. 87).

Sitkei, E. G., & Myers, C. F. Comparative structure of intellect in middle and lower-class four-year-olds of two ethnic groups. *Developmental Psychology,* 1969, **1,** 592-604.

Skeels, H. M. Adult status of children with contrasting early life experiences. *Monographs of the Society for Research in Child Development,* 1966, **31,** (3, whole No. 105).

Skeels, H. M., & Dye, H. B. A study of the effects of differential stimulation on mentally retarded children. *Proceedings of the American*

Association on Mental Deficiency, 1939, **44,** 114-136.

Templin, N. C. Relation of speech and language development to intelligence and socio-economic status. *Volta Review,* 1958, **60,** 331-334.

Terman, L. M., & Merrill, M. A. *Measuring intelligence: A guide to the administration of the new revised Stanford-Binet tests of intelligence.* New York: Houghton Mifflin, 1937.

Van Alstyne, D. The environment of three-year-old children: Factors related to intelligence and vocabulary tests. *Teachers College Contributions to Education,* 1929, No. 366.

Weikart D. P., & Lambie, D. Z. Preschool intervention through a home tutoring program. In J. Hellmuth (Ed.), *The disadvantaged child,* Vol. 2. Seattle: Special Child Publications, 1968.

Weikart, D. P., Lambie, D. Z., *et al.* Ypsilanti-Carnegie infant education project progress report. Department of Research and Development, Ypsilanti Public Schools, Ypsilanti, Michigan, 1969.

Werner, E. E., Simonian, K., & Smith, S. Reading achievement, language functioning and perceptual-motor development of 10-11 year olds. *Perceptual and Motor Skills,* 1967, **25,** 409-420.

Chapter 6

Early Enrichment in Infants

David P. Weikart and Dolores Z. Lambie

As a concept, compensatory education for disadvantaged children is in serious difficulty today. Spawned in the late fifties by the emerging desire that social and educational equality, as well as political equality, be considered legitimate goals for a democratic society, and nourished by the resurgence of the environment-oriented interaction theory of intelligence, compensatory education was seen as an answer to the achievement problems facing large numbers of youth from lower socioeconomic backgrounds. Pump in enough money, lower the teacher-pupil ratio, introduce new teaching techniques and new materials, be more responsive to the individual's needs for self-worth and any child can become successful in an educational system offering the technology and skills required for entry into the successful working and middle class groups.

But today, at the start of the seventies, assessments of the situation are uniformly pessimistic. A recent review of compensatory education results by Roger Freeman (1969), while overwhelmingly discouraging in its entirety, was most biting in its conclusion: "It is too much to hope that the latter-day alchemists in our public schools will see the futility of their quest in less time than it took their spiritual ancestors to accept the fact of life that gold can be found only where nature placed it."

A major criticism of the type of studies Freeman reviewed has been in the way the data were analyzed, a problem often generated by broad grouping of projects. The suggestion has been made that an appropriate, though biased, test of the concept of compensatory education would be to select only successful projects and examine them to see if the conclusions might be different. A recent review by the American Research Institute did just that. Hawkridge, Chalupsky, and Roberts (1968) reviewed data from compensatory programs covering preschool through twelfth grade for the period 1963-1968. They closely examined a sample of over 1000 projects from throughout the country nominated as successful compensatory education programs. They found only 21 programs which met a criterion of statistically significant data based on improved intellectual or academic functioning. Although there is little precedent for any prediction of success for those who might employ the particular intervention methods found to be effective by their inventors, these 21 studies have now been hailed by the US Office of Education as prototypes for adoption by other school systems (see the *It Works* series, US Office of Education).

As psychologists and educators have examined the outcome of compensatory education, one of the prime problems has been interpretation. Increasingly, the emphasis has shifted from the recognition of the importance of environment to a reaffirmation of the position of genetic prepotence in determining the general level of functioning that an individual attains (e.g., Jensen, 1969, writing in the *Harvard Review,* discussing performance on standardized intelligence tests; Kohlberg, 1968, in a review article for *Child Development* commenting on performance on Piagetian measures, or Chess, 1967, reviewing evidence on temperament in young children). Though couched in the newer terminology of interactional processes, this shift is a revival of the old nature-nurture debate; the outcome of this debate, however, will not alter the fact that the educator has more than enough room for major action, nor that he has the responsibility for effective programming.

For the educator the area offering the greatest "room for action" at this time is infant education, based on the belief that the essential framework and basis for intellectual growth is firmly established by age 4 (Bloom, 1964). Surprisingly, however, interest in infant education has been found primarily among psychologists concerned with delimiting theoretical child development issues and by social welfare workers committed to the provision of child-care facilities to permit women to work at outside jobs. Infant education as a potential method of altering basic intellectual growth patterns associated with specific socioeconomic class and ethnic child-rearing practices has not been widely explored.

Before turning to a description of a project in infant education designed to test the strength of this hypothesis, it is necessary to draw upon a key finding from preschool research regarding an important issue which has dominated preschool compensatory education for some time—the function of curriculum. This finding is essential because it shifts the focus of infant education from specific "activity" programs to more general problems of operation and broad goals.

PLACE OF CURRICULUM

Until recently, the main goal in early education research was to develop *the* curriculum for optimally affecting the general development of the child. The basic reason behind the failure of compensatory preschool education was assumed to be the inadequacy of treatment methods. In general, the major differences among the various curricula offered for use in preschools have been in the focus and amount of structure and in how this structure is thought to affect the general development of the child.

The dominant view in the early education field is that of the traditional nursery school educators. This position is best characterized as child-centered and permissive. Sears and Dowley (1963, p. 814) summarize the traditional methods as ". . . watching and waiting for the child's needs to emerge and (to) determine the timing of different activities . . ." The teacher provides the curriculum structure based upon her intuitive grasp of the child's stage of development. The best examples of this method are found in the classes of master teachers; what a master teacher does to achieve her results is a matter of personal expression, however.

Another point of view is held primarily by researchers new to the early education field. This position is best characterized as oriented toward structured programming, and it is usually based on a specific educational theory. A theoretical position might be derived from Piaget or Guilford, for example, where the primary goals would be cognitive and language development. The typical structured program is a carefully sequenced presentation of teacher-planned activities. While some structured programs may utilize traditional nursery school materials and activities, others turn directly to the task of teaching reading, writing, and arithmetic without even a nod toward traditional nursery school format. The structure may be derived from the curriculum materials themselves as well as from teacher commitment to a specific set of educational methods. In a structured program, the teacher is generally expected to understand how the activities will be used to achieve predetermined goals, and her teaching methods may range from the more traditional social controls to the newer behavior modification technology.

Since 1962, there have been a number of structured preschool education programs in operation (Deutsch, 1968; Gray & Klaus, 1969; Hodges, McCandless, & Spicker, 1967; Karnes, 1969; Klaus & Gray, 1968; Sprigle, 1967; Weikart, 1967). These projects have followed different child development theories and have been organized around diverse teaching strategies. The central theme of each, however, has been the imposition upon participating children of carefully designed sequences of activities. While these projects have not been uniformly successful, the data have been encouraging in terms of both their immediate measurable impact on general functional ability and the long-term gains in areas such as academic and social performance. Several of these projects were accepted as successful by the Hawkridge *et al.* (1968) study. While there is little theoretical agreement among these researchers as to what constitutes a good nursery school program, they do agree that systematic teaching is essential.

In an effort to determine which of two well-developed structured programs was most effective in meeting the needs of disadvantaged and functionally retarded children, the Ypsilanti Preschool Curriculum Demonstration Project was established in the fall of 1967. The programs selected were a cognitively oriented curriculum and a language training curriculum. The *cognitively oriented curriculum* had been developed over the past 5 years by the Ypsilanti Perry Preschool Project (Weikart, 1967). This curriculum is a carefully structured program specifically designed for disadvantaged children who are functionally re-tarded. It is based on methods of "verbal bombardment" of our own design, on principles of sociodramatic play as defined by Sarah Smilansky, and on child development principles derived from Piaget's theory. The *language training curriculum* was developed by Bereiter and Engelmann (1966) at the University of Illinois. This is a task-oriented program employing many tech-niques from foreign-language training; it includes the direct teaching of language, arithmetic, and reading. In order to complete the spectrum, a third program was established that would represent the traditional, or child-centered, approach to education. This program is called the *unit-based curriculum* and emphasizes the social-emotional goals and teaching methods of the traditional nursery school.

Much to our surprise, each of the three programs did unusually well on all criteria (Weikart, 1969). The findings indicated no differences among the three curricula on almost all of the many measures employed in program assessment, i.e., several intelligence tests (Stanford-Binet IQ gains by 3-year-olds of 27.5, 28.0, and 30.2 points, for example, in the first year), classroom observations, observations in free play settings, ratings of children by teachers and independent examiners, and evalua-tions by outside critics. These data have now been replicated with essentially the same findings at the end of the second year. The basic conclusion is that the operational conditions of an experimental project are far more potent in influencing the outcome than the particular curriculum employed. Specifically, we have derived four points regarding curriculum and the education of disadvantaged children.

Broad Curricula Are Equivalent

As far as various preschool curricula are concerned, children profit intellectually from any curriculum that is based on a wide range of experiences. In almost the sense that Chomsky (1966) uses in talking about the development of linguistic competence, a child has the potential to develop cognitive skills and good educational habits if he is presented with a situation which requires their expression. Kohlberg (1968) concludes that a child needs broad general forms of active experience for adequate development of his cognitive abilities; a variety of specific types of stimulation are more or less functionally equivalent for development. In short, no specific curriculum has the corner on effective stimuli, and children are powerful enough consumers to avail themselves of what the market offers.

The Curriculum Is for the Teacher Not the Child

The primary role of curriculum is (1) to focus the energy of the teacher on a systematic effort to help the individual child to learn, (2) to provide a rational and integrated base for deciding which activities to include and which to omit, and (3) to provide criteria for others to judge program effectiveness so that the teacher may be adequately supervised. The successful curriculum is one that permits this structuring of the *teacher* to guide her in the task of interaction with the theory she is applying, on the one hand, and the actual behavior of the child, on the other. An unsuccessful curriculum is one that permits the teacher to give her energies to areas unrelated to her interaction with the child within the theoretical framework or fails to give her clear guidelines for using her time in planning, in interaction with children, and in availing herself of critical supervision. The global and imprecise nature of the traditional preschool curriculum may explain why the master teacher's careful observation of the child and intuitive response to his needs is so successful, while the typical teacher, lacking structured guidelines, mistakes efficient organization at best and systematic neglect at worst for creative education.

The Selection or Development
of a Curriculum Is a Critical Decision

A curriculum that is too easy or limited in scope will not challenge the teachers and will fail in its function of demanding the teacher's maximum effort. In the long run, it may be that the current focus on "script" type curricula by some structure-oriented curriculum developers will produce as sterile a range of programs as the traditional curriculum people have produced, since the teacher in such programs is not given the room to make the curriculum actively her own. As effective as some of these programs currently are, they must stand the test of how teachers will respond after several years of following the "script." As Huxley (1965) said, "In the nature of things, machinery that is foolproof is also inspiration-proof, spontaneity-proof, and virtuosity-proof."

A staff must be free to develop or employ any dynamic curriculum that it believes will match the needs of the children so long as that curriculum provides adequately for staff involvement and facilitates the type of program operation desired. The process of creating and the creative application of *a* curriculum, not the particular curriculum selected or developed, is what is essential to success. In preschool education the process of reinventing the wheel is important not for the wheels produced but for the learning the process engenders.

The Staff Model Is More Important
Than the Particular Curriculum Employed

While competent administrative direction and a good curriculum are important to achieving success, staff involvement is crucial. The staff model employed must allow each individual to be creatively involved in the total operation. In an almost romantic sense, the human involvement of concerned teachers and staff is the key element in program success. To achieve such involvement, a project must provide adequate time for the staff to plan what they are going to do within the restrictions demanded by the particular curriculum, and it must provide for adequate critical supervision by experienced personnel.

Planning time gives the staff an opportunity to bring each child into clear focus, to schedule their own actions to help the child toward the next stage of development, and to debate the theory of the curriculum. Critical supervision must be provided to support the teachers in educational and operational problems, to give them "advice and comfort" in coping with the administrative structure, to facilitate their participation in decision making, and to administer in-service training in curriculum theory. The supervisor raises questions for the staff concerning the general operation of planning and teaching functions. She is the "referee" for problems within the team, bringing them out into the open rather than allowing them to be smoothed over. Since genuine program difficulties with individual children and among staff are the basis for program improvement, to smooth over problems is to avoid the opportunity they provide.

In summary, the major conclusion drawn from the preschool curriculum comparison study is that a curriculum is more important for the demands it places upon the project staff in terms of operation than for what it gives the child in terms of content. This finding permits different focus in an infant education program than would otherwise be possible. It makes the particular curriculum or activities of minor importance and permits clear program focus on the mother as the primary teacher of her own child with specific curriculum being her own invention. The role of the teacher is to assist and supervise the mother in this process.

INFANT EDUCATION

The commitment to an infant education program is based on our experience in longitudinal preschool research and programming for 3- and 4-year-olds. We found that while we were successful with about half of our preschool children, we were not achieving the desired rate of growth in all of the children involved. One solution is to focus on preventative programs and start educational intervention before deficits are found. Pasamanick and Knoblock (1961) and Bayley (1965) using general developmental tests, have reported no measurable developmental differences between groups of normal infants in the first 15 months.

The format of the infant education project is home teaching rather than, for example, day care, with the mother, her child, and the teacher as the educational unit. This format was selected because of successful experiences with home teaching over the years in our preschool programs (Weikart, 1967; Weikart & Lambie, 1968). In addition, there is a strong staff commitment to the critical importance of the mother's relationship with her child in establishing the foundation of the child's personality, his general capacities and his habits in relating to the world. As long as the family structure is the essential socializing agent in our society and the family unit is accepted as the core social component, public policy and public practice must be designed to enhance that relationship, not destroy it.

Overview

The Ypsilanti Carnegie Infant Education Project was established in January, 1968, and is funded by the Carnegie Corporation, National Institute of Public Health, and the Ypsilanti Public Schools (Lambie & Weikart, 1969). The project is based on two assumptions: (1) Preventative programming must start earlier than current preschool efforts since the essential framework for intellectual growth is completed by age 3; (2) preventative intervention has unusual potential for success when provided as a home teaching program for both the mother and her infant. Early infancy is a time of extremely rapid intellectual and physical growth, and it is the period when primary emotional relationships are established; most mothers from all cultural backgrounds hold high hopes for their infants and welcome assistance in attaining their goals.

The purpose of the project is to assess the effectiveness of systematic intervention by public school teachers, starting at the period of infancy, in preventing the intellectual deficits commonly found in children from disadvantaged populations. In order to control some of the important variables, four groups have been established: an experimental group; a contrast group; and two control groups. The experimental group utilizes home teaching by public school teachers as the method of program operation. In this plan, a public school teacher goes into the home to work with the mother and her infant once each week for about an hour. During the visit the teacher expresses her genuine interest in the mother and what she is doing with the child, especially as it relates to language, motoric development, and cognitive growth. The mother is helped to become aware of the infant's development in each of these key areas by learning to observe her child closely, and she is encouraged to respond to the child as each small step of growth evolves. In this process, the mother becomes deeply involved in the child's development. Specifically, the visits are organized around five points: individualized programming for each mother-child dyad; development of the mother's teaching style, language style, and control techniques; and direct tutoring of the child. Since the overall goal is to help each mother become an effective teacher of her child, the project staff strongly rejects the development of a standardized "script" of activities for the teacher, the mother, or the child. The home teaching process is carefully supervised and developed in a systematic fashion by the project staff.

The contrast group employs home visits by paraprofessionals from the community. The focus of these visits is adult attention for the child and service to the family. The "intuitive wisdom" of the paraprofessional is the basis of the work with the family. They receive professional supervision with regard to operational problems but not with regard to curriculum content.

One control group is a traditional no-treatment group receiving only the same testing as the other groups. The second control group is a no-treatment, no-testing group created from those families who, for reasons beyond their control, had to drop out from one of the above three groups. In every case, the initial testing has been completed, and no further testing will be done with the family and child until the project has been completed.

The groups are created by random assignment of mother-child dyads from the available disadvantaged families of the Ypsilanti school district. The groups are further subdivided by age of entry into the project. The youngsters are phased into the project at 3, 7, and 11 months of age to provide information on the effect of entry age on program impact. The groups are also controlled for race and sex so far as this is possible.

Dynamics of Working in the Home. Teachers working in the homes of disadvantaged families must accept a role different from that assumed when working in traditional classroom or clinical settings. Professionally, teachers are trained to work with groups that are basically captive audiences making the sacrifice and effort to be present and assuming "low power" positions, i.e., sitting at desks, answering roll calls, and performing to teacher expectations. In addition, classroom teachers seldom have their performance judged in any immediate way other than being "liked" or "disliked" by their students. Only occasionally is long-term achievement by students introduced as a possible consideration of teaching effectiveness. Home teaching, on the other hand, demands a very different performance on the part of the teacher; acceptance of a position of low power, immediate critical evaluation of teaching, and adjustment to economic and social differences are all required.

The teacher is a guest in the home of a mother. As a guest, the teacher must sit where told to sit and put up with many inconveniences, e.g., dirt, bugs, disease, poor heating, lack of work space, lack of access to teaching supplies, assorted visitors viewing the teaching, summary dismissal by the mother, and cancellations of appointments by the mother. In all of this the teacher basically assumes a position of low power.

In addition, the mother does an immediate evaluation of the teacher's performance during the working session. In the classroom the teacher is seldom judged in areas other than discipline and classroom management. In the home, trial-and-error teaching is not well received and negative reaction is immediate to teaching failure. The teacher must demonstrate that she can tap the child's ability, handle teaching situations correctly, and explain why something did or did not work. If she fails in any of these categories, she seldom receives a second chance unless the mother is convinced of the teacher's expertise.

It is essential that the teacher neither make moral judgements nor show surprise, disgust, or rejection of aspects of the social, cultural, and moral make-up of the family which are apparent to her even though she does not try to become aware of them. The teacher who focuses her interest on the child and on the mother as the child's teacher is more likely to reach the goals for improvement in the child and changes in the mother than the one who is overly absorbed in such things as cleanliness and presence or absence of fathers. Since culturally different situations do occur, however, the teacher needs ideas on how to handle them as well as a few well chosen rules, such as: "Do not enter the house if a child answers the door. Ask the child to get his mother, then wait outside until she knows you are present."

The key element of concern for the project staff is that the mother stimulate and support the infant's growth. This single and narrow focus makes her role as teacher palatable to the mother over the long period of contact. Only those things which have a direct bearing on the infant's participation in the teaching session are brought up with the mother. For example, if the baby has diaper rash and is fussy and cannot sit for the activities, the teacher might mention using cornstarch and changing diapers frequently. If the rash is severe, the teacher would encourage the mother to keep her appointment at the well-baby clinic and to ask for suggestions from the doctor, or she would suggest that the mother call the visiting nurse assigned to her for help in clearing up the rash. In any case, the teacher constantly reinforces for the mother the idea that her only concern is the intellectual development of the child, and that the mother is the child's real teacher. (This position of only educational concern is possible in this southeastern Michigan community because of the extensive agency service available to all families with need. Such a position is not feasible in centers operated by the Foundation in Mississippi, for example.)

While home teaching is not a traditional form of education, the advantages of working with mothers in their own homes are significant. The most obvious advantage is the convenience for the mothers especially those with large families. Since the teacher goes to the mother, she does not have to worry about transportation, baby sitters, her clothes, shoes, or hair. While these things may seem mundane, to some mothers these factors are insurmountable hurdles. After the first few contacts with the mother the strangeness of having a teacher in the house is dispelled and the teaching sessions become a natural part of the week. In fact, the sessions frequently are the neighborhood status symbol, an almost irresistible attraction for other mothers, grandmothers, or landlords.

A second advantage is the direct relevance of the sessions to the *mother and child.* Some mothers have a tendency either not to consider or to discard quickly information about child rearing provided by media such as TV and books. Because most of the information does not apply to their experiences with children and beliefs about child rearing, it is difficult for them to translate into everyday practice and often improperly used. A valuable result of having the teaching sessions in the mother's home is that many mothers readily include the content of the sessions in their family life. Sharing information about the child's growth, finding out that suitable toys can be made from common and inexpensive items, learning ways to occupy and manage other preschoolers who are at home, and discussing child-management problems all seem to generate a more favorable climate for change.

A third advantage is the specific real information the teacher has about the mother and child. Being in the house, where the child and mother spend most of their time, forces the teacher to be aware of environmental factors that may influence a mother's interaction with her infant. For example, in some homes the mothers are under vigorous pressure from family members not to involve themselves in anything as silly as talking to a baby. Making regular visits to the home makes it easier for the teacher to support the mother, to talk with the family about child development, and to answer the loaded questions presented by those in the family with the most negative attitudes. In most cases the minimum result of the teaching sessions is a lessening of pressure on the mother and this may even induce others to try supportive interaction with the child.

A fourth advantage is the opportunity to establish a meaningful link between the schools and families that do not easily trust such social agents. Many mothers initially seem to put the teachers on trial: Sink or swim, prove yourself valuable, and your intentions honorable. These mothers allow us to visit without any intention either of making the situation easy or of investing themselves in the session. This kind of mother would be inaccessible and resistant to most educational endeavors, but by being in *her* house, not the school house, the teacher at least gets a chance to demonstrate her ability to be relevant. Some of these families are known to every agency within the county, and after excessive amounts of time, energy, and money have been spent for professional staff, either the agencies have given up, or the family has closed its door. However, in most instances these mothers have been able to establish relationships with our teachers that result in positive changes; although these changes come about very slowly, they seem to be permanent, as shown by the mothers' behavior with new babies in their families.

ROLE OF CURRICULUM

From the curriculum comparison project reported in the first section of this chapter, the conclusion was drawn that the particular activities employed in any curriculum are not as important as the way in which the curriculum is implemented by the staff. The construction of an intervention curriculum for disadvantaged infants is an entirely different task from the usual psychological study of normal or abnormal infant development. The teacher's assignment is to enter into the mother-infant transaction to modify, when necessary, the "naturally" occuring dynamics and produce a process supportive of both the child and the mother. The teacher employs what she finds in the initial relationship to guide the mother in positive responses to the observed growth of the child. This interrelationship, based upon the actual growth of the infant, permits a powerful affectional bond between the mother and child and creates optimal circumstances for the child's mastery of the environment.

Because a successful program must be carefully individualized for each mother-child dyad, the essential condition for effective home teaching by the teacher is the development of an understanding of the mother's and infant's behavior and the infant's stage of development, followed by a program of action to facilitate growth based on that understanding. Since the main goal of home teaching is to enable each mother to become an effective teacher of her child, the teacher is interested in influencing the mother in terms both of her perception of her child and of the information available to her for choice of action. In order to accomplish these things in the teaching sessions, the following criteria for curricula were derived.

(1) *The curriculum must provide basic information about child development.* Since the curriculum is a tool to help the teachers focus on language acquisition, cognitive development and motoric skills as part of the mother-child relationship, considerable time was spent reviewing various developmental scales with special attention given to sensory-motor development as stressed by Piaget. The Uzgiris-Hunt Scales, based on Piagetian concepts, seemed to provide the most inclusive framework on which to build activities. This matrix gives the teacher the *structure* she needs to systematically make the small, everyday decisions necessary to sustain the child's interest and growth.

Piaget's descriptions of stages in development facilitate explanations to mothers about gross sequences or changes in the child's behavior. For example, in one stage of the sensory-motor period, it is common for the child no longer to want the mother to activate a toy or show him how it works; he would rather try all the schemas available to him for discovery. The teacher can use the information she has about tertiary circular reactions to emphasize the naturalness of this behavior as a part of learning. Many times this approach has an impact on control techniques as well. If the mother does not think of the child as stubborn or naughty, she would not punish him for pushing her hand away from the toy. This misinterpretation of a child's response is frequently the impetus for parent-child battles; it also puts a damper on the child's curiosity and his vigorous pursuit of discovery.

(2) *The curriculum must be adjustable.* It is quite clear that although it is comfortable to have a list of activities in hand, teachers are much more effective if the curriculum is not too restrictive but leaves room for creativity and adaptation to needs of individual children and mother-child pairs. This element of elasticity does not refute the necessity for structure. Most teachers feel a need for direction. The process of being an effective teacher includes specific activities for teacher, mother and child which intensify home teaching. Therefore, curriculum activities must be stated in such a way that both the *content* of

the activity and the *expected behavior* are clear *without restricting* the teacher in making decisions appropriate to each mother and child. Rather than consider what function a specific toy performs best, or which activity and which toy go together, the teacher can select and use a large variety of objects or toys to elicit the desired behaviors. In addition, separate lists or discussions of useful methods and techniques must be available so that teachers can choose an alternative method to maximize the responsiveness of the mother and child.

(3) *The curriculum must not overshadow the teacher.* Attention to the involvement and interest of the teacher is as important as any theoretical decision in the program. The curriculum cannot be so specific that it becomes a boring, mechanical application of activities applied to the child like an ointment. It must enhance what the teacher intuitively knows or can observe about children. A curriculum theory just difficult enough to create disequilibrium on the part of the teacher will sustain her interest and produce changes in her thinking and approach. Involved teachers have a desire to try, even when the situation is bleak, and are able to be creative within the chosen framework.

(4) *The curriculum must provide the teacher with some criteria for assessing progress.* If criteria are not provided, the concerned teacher will create her own. It is necessary to personally know, session by session, what is successful, when the child is learning, and where to go next, if something is unsuccessful, the teacher must have enough generally sequenced information about development to permit change in content or in the developmental level at which the activities are performed. Frequently, good criteria prevent teachers from falling into periods of inactivity that result from blaming themselves, the administration, the curriculum, or the child for failure.

(5) *The curriculum must be an adequate vehicle for delivering services that accomplish the goals.* A successful curriculum will provide an easily observable series of behaviors that teachers can use to demonstrate developmental progression to the mothers. One implicit objective of the home-teaching program has

been to make mothers aware that development is not just composed of dramatic learnings like walking, taking that first step or drinking from a cup, but that learning and growing are a parade of small accomplishments and understandings that make the grander ones possible. The teacher does not undermine the mother's pride in milestone accomplishments; rather, when a mother excitedly shares the fact that her child is drinking from a cup, the teacher can summarize some of the behaviors that preceded this milestone: attending, focusing on objects, reaching, grasping, holding, and putting things in the mouth. In this manner the teacher provides a view of development that reflects not only daily or weekly changes but a continuum of cumulative behaviors.

RESULTS

While a number of instruments are being employed to assess the impact of this program upon the infant and the mother, the results are preliminary at best. Reported in Tables I through IV are the data from the first 4 months of intervention employing the Bayley Scales of Infant Development. Data from various teacher report forms, attitude measures, and some measures based on "Attention to Stimuli" are not available at this time.

In this analysis[1] the dependent variable was the 4-month Bayley retest score, and the entering Bayley was used as a covariate to control for entering differences. A two-factor analysis of variance design was used, having group and age as the factors. The data matrix containing cell sizes is presented in the following tabulation:

	Months		
	3	7	11
Experimental	9	9	8
Contrast	9	7	4
Control	5	9	7

[1] Prepared by Dennis Deloria, Supervisor, Data Group, High/Scope Educational Research Foundation, Ypsilanti, Michigan.

To answer the questions of most interest, the between groups degrees of freedom were divided into group main effects and age within group simple main effects. Each of the overall F tests contained two degrees of freedom, and orthogonal contrasts of importance were selected a priori to use up each independent source of variance within the overall tests (see Tables II and IV).

In order to achieve the flexibility necessary to accomodate this nonstandard design involving tests of simple main effects, tests of specific contrasts, and unequal cell N, a multiple-regression computer program was used which allows the user to specify particular models and F tests (program REGRAN; Veldman, 1967). The model coefficients were adjusted for unequal cell sizes to insure orthogonality between tests.

Based on the data presented in the tables, there is no statistical evidence that immediate short-term results, as measured by the Bayley scales, favor either the paraprofessional or teacher-operated intervention programs over regular home care.

TABLE I   Group Means[a]

Group	Months			Combined ages
	3	7	11	
Experimental				
Test 1	93.0	99.0	101.6	97.7
Test 2	97.1	115.8	100.5	104.5
Difference	+4.1	+16.8	−1.1	+6.8
Contrast				
Test 1	99.0	92.7	105.5	98.1
Test 2	103.0	115.7	105.3	107.9
Difference	+4.0	+23.0	−0.2	+9.8
Control				
Test 1	92.0	82.8	101.9	91.3
Test 2	87.0	92.4	99.7	93.6
Difference	−5.0	+9.6	−2.2	+2.3

[a] Bayley Mental DQ Score.

TABLE II   Analysis of Covariance Results[a]

Source of variance	df	F	p[b]	R[2c]
Between				
Group main effects	2	1.754	N.S.	.036
Experimental vs. contrast	1	$<$1	N.S.	.004
Experimental + contrast vs. control	1	3.129	$<$.10	.032
Age within experimental	2	2.741	$<$.10	.057
Linear component	1	$<$1	N.S.	.001
Quadratic component	1	5.370	$<$.05	.056
Age within contrast	2	2.607	$<$.10	.054
Linear component	1	$<$1	N.S.	.000
Quadratic component	1	5.176	$<$.05	.054
Age within control	2	$<$1	N.S.	.017
Linear component	1	$<$1	N.S.	.004
Quadratic component	1	1.239	N.S.	.013
Within				
Error	57	–	–	.589
Covariate	1	20.202	.01	.209

[a]Bayley Mental DQ Score.

[b]None of the overall F test reach significance, so the contrast F tests are only indicative of trends in the data and should be interpreted with caution.

[c]Squared multiple-correlation coefficient. ($R^2 \times 100$ = percent of variance accounted for by each F test.)

There is some indication that age effects are important, at least in the mental scales. The results demonstrate major shifts, for all three groups, in mental development during the 7- to 11-month range. Also apparent is the general stability, irrespective of intervention, during the 11- to 15-month range, at least as measured by the Bayley.

A general qualitative impression of the response to the project is that both the experimental and contrast group children are progressing more rapidly than the control children. While examiners, testing blind, report amazing responsiveness among the first two groups, they are frequently surprised at how well a control group child scores when he did not seem to respond that well during the testing.

TABLE III   Group Means[a]

| Group | | Months | | Combined |
	3	7	11	ages
Experimental				
Test 1	92.3	96.3	103.4	97.3
Test 2	98.8	103.2	99.9	100.7
Difference	+6.5	+6.9	−3.5	+3.4
Contrast				
Test 1	102.8	99.7	109.3	103.2
Test 2	109.3	106.5	109.5	108.5
Difference	+6.5	+6.8	+0.2	+5.3
Control				
Test 1	91.0	94.0	108.4	98.1
Test 2	97.6	98.6	101.0	99.1
Difference	+6.6	+4.6	−7.4	+1.0

[a] Bayley Motor DQ Score.

While changes in functioning as measured by the Bayley scales are not the only dependent variables being studied, they are among the most important. At this time the data are too preliminary to do more than report them. If these initial trends are maintained for the remainder of the 16 months of intervention, however, the data should be of considerable interest.

CONCLUSIONS

With the project now a year in operation, it is possible to see the potential of home teaching. Perhaps the most important observation is that the process of a teacher, a mother, and an infant *getting ready* to learn together is even more critical than what is actually done. To be sure, the teacher must have ideas and

TABLE IV   Analysis of Covariance Results[a]

Source of variance	df	F	p	R^{2b}
Between				
Group main effects	2	<1	N.S.	.024
Experimental vs. contrast	1	<1	N.S.	.012
Experimental + contrast vs. control	1	<1	N.S.	.012
Age within experimental	2	<1	N.S.	.011
Linear component	1	<1	N.S.	.005
Quadratic component	1	1	N.S.	.007
Age within contrast	2	<1	N.S.	.002
Linear component	1	<1	N.S.	.002
Quadratic component	1	<1	N.S.	.000
Age within control	2	<1	N.S.	.007
Linear component	1	<1	N.S.	.005
Quadratic component	1	<1	N.S.	.002
Within				
Error	57	–	–	.718
Covariate	1	17.353	.01	.219

[a] Bayley Motor DQ Score.

[b] Squared multiple-correlation coefficient. ($R^2 \times 100$ = percent of variance accounted for by each F test.)

"expertise" to assist the mother and infant in learning, but that is a long way from simply providing a family with a series of exercises like those presented in an infant development manual. The process of helping the family prepare for learning is still a fairly intuitive one on the part of the teacher. It includes great persistence by the teacher in focusing the mother's attention on the educational problems at hand. The process includes absolute flexibility in lesson plans to meet the mother half way in whatever direction is necessary to help her focus on her child. In short, the human relationship, in an almost romantic sense, is the essential condition for any educational growth. Without this relationship, nothing will occur.

Then there has been the gradual realization that child development "theory," no matter how sophisticated, does not have as much to say as desired about specific children and their mothers. A teacher must be ready and willing to step slowly through the great distances that separate landmarks in the child's development. Using a baby's table banging as the occasion to introduce "bang bang" vocalizations would be an example of "making do" within a real teaching situation. A teacher must blend the needs of the mother with the needs of the infant in such a way as to maximize the learning opportunity for both.

Whether or not the basic hypothesis of this research, that education in early infancy can prevent intellectual and educational handicaps, will be found to be true, the essential fact at this point is that disadvantaged families are willing to accept infant education. The job at hand is to do this effectively.

ACKNOWLEDGMENTS

The infant research was partially supported by the Carnegie Corporation and the Department of Health, Education, and Welfare, Public Health Service, Grant No. 1 R01 MH17462-01 JP. The preschool research was partially supported by the US Office of Education, ESEA Title III Grant, Project 68-5636.

REFERENCES

Bayley, N. Comparison of mental and motor test scores for ages 1-15 months by sex, birth order, race, geographical location and education of parents. *Child Development,* 1965, **36,** 379-411.

Bereiter, C., & Engelmann, S. *Teaching disadvantaged children in preschool.* Englewood Cliffs, N. J.: Prentice-Hall, 1966.

Bloom, B. *Stability and change in human characteristics.* New York: Wiley, 1964.

Chess, S. Temperament in the normal infant. In J. Hellmuth (Ed.), *Exceptional infant,* Vol. 1. Seattle: Special Child Publication, 1967, Pp. 143-162.

Chomsky, N. *Cartesian linguistics.* New York: Harper & Row, 1966.

Deutsch, M. Institute for developmental studies: Interim progress report, Part II. New York University, 1968.

Freeman, R. The alchemists in our public schools, In J. Hellmuth (Ed.),

Disadvantaged child, Vol. 3 *Compensatory education: A national debate.* New York: Brunner/Mazel, 1970.

Gray, S. W., & Klaus, R. The early training project: A seventh year report. John F. Kennedy Center for Research on Education and Human Development, George Peabody College, 1969.

Hawkridge, D., Chalupsky, A., & Roberts, A. A study of selected exemplary programs for the education of disadvantaged children. American Institutes for Research in the Behavioral Sciences, Palo Alto, California, 1968.

Hodges, W., McCandless, B., & Spicker, H. The development and evaluation of a diagnostically based curriculum for preschool psycho-socially deprived children. U. S. Department of Health, Education and Welfare, Office of Education, Bureau of Research, Washington, D. C., 1967.

Huxley, A. Human potentialities. In R. Farson (Ed.), *Science and human affairs.* Palo Alto, Calif.: Science & Behavior Books, 1965.

Jensen, A. How much can we boost I.Q. and scholastic achievement? *Harvard Educational Review,* Winter, 1969.

Karnes, M. B. Research and development program on preschool disadvantaged children. U. S. Department of Health, Education and Welfare, Office of Education, Bureau of Research, Washington, D. C., 1969.

Klaus, R., & Gray, S. W. The early training project for disadvantaged children: A report after five years. *Monographs of the Society for Research in Child Development,* 1968, Serial No. 120, Vol. 33, No. 4.

Kohlberg, L. Early education: A cognitive-developmental view. *Child Development,* 1968, **39,** 1013-1062.

Lambie, D. Z. & Weikart, D., Ypsilanti-Carnegie infant education project. In J. Hellmuth (Ed.) *Disadvantaged child,* Vol. 3. New York: Brunner/Mazel, 1970.

Pasamanick, B. & Knoblock, H. Epidemiologic studies on the complications of pregnancy and the birth process. In C. Caplan (Ed.), *Prevention of mental disorders in children.* New York: Basic Books, 1961, Pp. 74-94.

Sears P. S., & Dowley, E. M. Research on teaching in the nursery school. In N. L. Gage (Ed.), *Handbook of research on teaching.* Chicago: Rand McNally, 1963, Pp. 811-864.

Sprigle, H. Curriculum development and innovations in learning materials for early childhood education. Paper read at the Southern Conference on Early Childhood Education, University of Georgia, March 1967.

Veldman, D. *Fortran programming for the behavioral sciences.* New York: Holt, Rinehart & Winston, 1967.

Weikart, D. Preliminary results from a longitudinal study of disadvantaged preschool children. Paper presented at the convention of the Council for Exceptional Children, St. Louis, 1967.

Weikart, D. A comparative study of three preschool curricula. Paper presented at the biennial meeting of the Society for Research in Child Development, Santa Monica, California, March 1969.

Weikart, D., and Lambie, D. Z. Preschool intervention through a home teaching program. In J. Hellmuth (Ed.), *The disadvantaged child,* Vol. 2. Seattle: Special Child Publications, 1968.

Weikart, D., & Lambie, D. Z. Ypsilanti-Carnegie infant education project progress report. Ypsilanti Public Schools, Ypsilanti, Michigan, 1969.

Chapter 7

Discussion: Infant Education as Viewed by a Psychologist | *Jerome S. Bruner*

I would like if possible to extract from the varied papers some general themes. The process of extraction is, of course, subject to one's own biased information processing.

A first general consensus is that there is much important impact on intellectual growth controlled by what takes place during earlier years of life than had before seemed likely. While there are proverbs to this effect, the view has not always been accepted as a basis for policy. It is now being accepted, it seems to me, as a matter to be seriously considered in social policy decisions. We are at a stage now where we believe that it is necessary to intervene publicly in the early years of life where necessary, and I think now it would be fair to say that the early years of life begin at birth.

There are various forms of evidence that have been proposed in support of this view. One of them is the importance of social class differences and their impact on growth very early in the child's life. The differential rate of failure between the lower-class and the middle-class child, which my colleague Dr. Kagan properly makes much of, reflects treatment in the early years and poses a new form of crisis for a society where technical competency is more important than it has ever been in the history of man's efforts to cope. There is also frequent citation of Bloom's conclusion that an enormous amount of the variance in intellectual capacity is committed before schooling ever begins, although many deep questions can be raised about such correlations. They may be too exclusively tied to tests of school-bound activities, and the argument goes that there are other ways than schoollike ones of being intelligent.

There is, by the way, a great deal of latent nondiscussion of the subject of the reversibility of what happens in the first year of life. To what extent is the first year so buffered that you can feel reasonably safe about it, providing there are no extreme events like battering or neglect-in-the-closet. How much matters before the development of language? We simply do not know. I would only want to specify one thing. I have been engaged for the last couple of years in very close, almost ethological, studies of the development of various forms of skill in infancy, and it is quite plain that a great deal of confidence, zest, and verve seem to be developing by virtue of the child mastering certain kinds of skills. It is very difficult for me as a psychologist to doubt that those accesses of competence that seem to be so satisfying to the child do not matter at all later on. They seem to be a platform which the child can then mount for higher ascents.

There are several interpretations as to why early childhood (leaving aside early infancy) matters so much. Although there is absence of consensus, there does seem to be convergence. There is first of all the reasonable position so elegantly stated by Dr. Mason that during that early period there is a kind of learning to learn that is tremendously important; there are also certain forms of nonspecific learning that have to do with the maintenance of attention, with the development of what Kagan called the mobilization of cognitive schemata in the face of novelty and unpredictability. Others suggest that some of this nonspecific learning may result from constancy in the family environment over time which finally produces, by the force of the constancy of the environment, certain forms of mental functioning. These may be hindered by the slum child's more disordered environment; but it is not just a question of skills, specific or otherwise, for the child also learns to conform to a family culture, which may in turn reflect a class culture.

There is also the view that part of the importance of the early period comes from the fact that it produces differentials in achievement by inflicting defeat on the young of some social classes more than others, giving them an attitude of hopelessness while other children build strategies based on the hope of success. The differential is, so to speak, from the middle down, rather than the middle up.

It is also being pointed out increasingly that there is a genetic factor that may operate, and it seems to me that the evidence on balance favors this view. The presence of a genetic factor should support neither despair nor racism. There is probably some advantage in the statistical sense to being born at the more successful end of the socioeconomic ladder, both culturally and genetically. But there is still a problem in assuring the realization of one's genetic constitution or of interfering with it. So that while it is quite true that we vary genetically as do all other species, this is certainly not an argument *against* assisting and supporting growth. Indeed, it is an argument for *more* help for any who might start off with less genetic capacity—an expression that means among other things that more instruction is needed to reach a particular level.

A certain malaise with our social order has also been expressed, that there is something rotten in the society that prevents us thinking properly about the young, particularly the young of the poor, but also about the rights of the young and of their mothers to receive aid. The issue is presented as a moral and political one that will doubtless become increasingly important over the coming years. It is urged that we look not only at the psychological question of why a poor or a black child does not cope well in school, but also look at the very structure of our society that created this condition. It can only be hoped that this malaise grows in conviction and in constructiveness.

Plainly, too, there is a need to provide the young child with a rich variety of social and nonsocial events in his environment with which to interact. This, it seems to me, was quite properly stated by Mason in a biological context. In respect to primate evolution, what is most striking is the enormous proliferation of substitution rules in ways of coping with the environment, until finally in man we come to the substitution system par excellence—language. The different ways in which one can say or do virtually the same thing, achieve the same objective, are almost limitless. Provision for an opportunity to use this open capacity, to get away from the stereotype, the boredom, the homogeneity of a poor environment is tremendously important. It is striking, by the way, in what a variety of forms this point emerged in the different papers that have been presented.

I would like to make one point in this connection. It has to do with the issue of a growing human being's rights. We tend too often, it seems to me, to think of early assistance to growth either in the metaphor of "intervention" or of "remedy." If we take seriously what has been said about the condition necessary to achieve full potential growth in a human organism, then we shall have to abandon both metaphors. We must assist the young to grow, whether by day care, home visits, or other means; if we do not, they will not achieve their fullness as men and women. It is not "intervention" or "cure," it is the provision of the kind of environment necessary for growth, whatever one's parents' skin color, religion, pocketbook, origin, or genetic structure.

With respect to types of day care, home visitings, etc., I was made particularly aware by Dave Weikart's presentation that there are many different ways in which we can operate effectively. I think these are false dichotomies that divide us, like day care vs. home care, as if one were good to the other's detriment. Even in a kibbutz it is not at all clear who is the caretaker and who is the mother, particularly when mothers are so often around the nursery, "working" there or just "being" there. Admittedly, it is still too early to be doctrinaire about curriculum. It is quite plain that there are many modes of instruction. Levenstein's (1968) studies using visiting "toy demonstrators" in homes suggests that a great deal of helpful interaction takes the form that David and Appell (1970) have written about of developing a relationship between mother and child by having both orient toward a common plaything rather than directly toward each other. Yet, this does not mean that a "third object" approach is necessary or "better." And so on down a list of "opposites."

Many people today have urged that we give up the idea of the school as the sole instrument, or even the principal instrument of education. We now take a much broader view of development and of the role of the educational process in it. We plainly need a theory of education whose pedagogy is not schoolbound.

Finally, I do not want to add to the various lists that have been proposed concerning the basic underlying processes in the care of the young, the underprivileged young particularly. Rather, mention of just four or five very general trends that seem to me present in everybody's list seems in order.

The first is that there is an enormous influence exerted by the caretaker, be it mother, teacher, or whoever the person who is usually there. Is it the role of an accessible model, or as John Bowlby (1969) has recently proposed, is it that the caretaker provides a basis for reciprocal relationship that allows the infant to develop rules for getting on generally? While the importance of reciprocity is universally granted, *most contemporary theories of intellectual or cognitive development leave the matter out of account.* I include my own theories in this condemnation. Indeed, it may be the case that the first regularity that we represent is another person. It may be the model for later representations of the environment.

Second, virtually everybody agrees that on the working level there is a *small* gradual acquisition of skill and competence on a day-to-day basis during infancy and childhood. Life and growth do not consist of monumental milestones and boundaries with memorable crossings. Yet, most of the theories of development upon which we must lean consist principally of emphases upon great leaps forward at rare occasions, with the rest involving a catching up of the fragments. This is true of the Piagetian, the Freudian, and other grand theoretical outlooks. In fact, skills are mastered on a day-by-day basis, and once mastered, they permit the development of new skills, which in turn serve, so to speak, as

the modules for the development of still higher skills. It is this
process of solidifying and developing competence in depth, using
what one has learned for new ventures, that gives continuity to
growth and slowly endows the learner with confidence in his
ability to cope. This is one reason, I suspect, why David Weikart's
different compensatory programs have all worked well, since one
feature in common between his Piagetian program, the efforts of
his master teachers, and the rest, is that all of them let the child
use a skill to go on to something else, to gain from it a sense of
mastery and self-confidence. Again, the theoretical framework in
which we work is not adequate to the guidance required nor does
it encourage the research required. I sense all of us feel this lack.

A third general consensus: There is an enormous contribution
to cognitive development from factors that, on the surface, are
anything but traditionally cognitive. They are, instead, diffuse
affective factors. Kagan discussed confidence, the capacity to
control one's environment, hope in the future—these are necessary conditions for cognitive growth. I recall an old study by
Bloom and Broder (1950) in which they showed that even in a
simple two-choice problem-solving situation, one of the less
demanding procedures to which we submit our subjects, what
kind of strategy was used was determined to an astonishing
extent by whether the subject believed a solution was or was not
possible. Our stupidity and our cleverness in more situations than
we know may be as much a matter of heart as of mind. I would
beg of you not to remain content with the division of our subject
into two volumes, one called "affective factors," and the other
"cognitive factors." What we have discussed suggests at least that
we cut off the front binding of the second volume, the back one
of the first, and sew the two together. Some of you may even
recognize the volumes to which I refer.

Fourth, I think we are beginning to agree that the idea
we started with a few years ago, the idea of an enriched environment that gives the child a rich surround, puts the child in
the position of a passive consumer, and is in error as an emphasis

One study after another shows that for a child to learn, he must go it on his own, operate on his own activation. It is this activation that must be supported. This can be illustrated in terms of first walking. The child who has confidence that he is going to be helped or supported in walking will take the risk. Even the child who has been suffering during his first 10 months with spherocytosis, operating at 50% oxygen level, will risk an unsupported step if he knows there is some help forthcoming. But for all the help, he will not make progress until he tries it on his own, under the government of his own intentions. We must talk about enriched *people,* not enriched *environments.* Our interventions must enable children to become richer in their intentions, not in their environmental possessions. Our particular research group agrees that one of the single most important matters in the care of the young is the maturing of intention, providing opportunity for the emergence of intentional, goal-directed, goal-seeking, means-analyzing human beings. The objective is not passive consumers of enriched environments but active producers of their "own thing."

Finally, it has been clear in all the papers, as it is clear in reviewing the literature, that little can be done for a human being with a "one-shot" intervention. One has to work at it. Head Start alone does not work, if afterward the child is dumped into a punishing school experience. When we build an expectancy, build a skill, we incur a responsibility for nurturing it. It may, in some instances, be a compounding of evils to open the child's vulnerabilities, and then disappoint or dump him. If we are to be effective in helping disadvantaged children cope better, it is their life cycle that must be dealt with, not their preschool or their nursery or their street life. This is why we need diverse forms of care and can hardly tolerate quarrels about this form vs. that form on ideological grounds rather than evidence. Likely as not, day care will improve home care, will in turn improve the designing of toys, will improve how parents observe children, and so on. The important thing is to get going. We must surely praise the attitude that though the first programs may not happen to be our *preferred* ones, nonetheless, we try to make them as good as possible, knowing that we shall surely go on from there.

REFERENCES

Bloom, B. S., & Broder, L. J. Problem-solving processes of college students. *Educational Monographs*, 1950, Suppl.

Bowlby, J. *Attachment and loss,* Vol. 1. New York: Basic Books, 1969.

David, M., & Appell, G. Mother-child interaction and its impact on the child. In J. A. Ambrose (Ed.), *Stimulation in early infancy.* New York: Academic Press, 1970.

Levenstein, P. Aiding cognitive growth in disadvantaged preschoolers. Progress Report, February 1968, Children's Bureau Research Project R-300, Family Service Association of Nassau County, Inc., New York.

Chapter 8

Discussion: Infant Education as Viewed by a Public Program Manager | *Richard E. Orton*

I am not a scientist, but rather an artist—I engage in the occult art of management. How many times I wish it were an exact science! My job is to help see to it that the hundreds of millions of dollars that has been entrusted to us by Congress to operate Project Head Start is well spent—easy to describe, but impossible to do to everyone's satisfaction.

Each of us, those who are managers and those who are scientists in our weaker moments, occasionally think of the other in myths. I suspect that many scientists consider many of us muscle-headed bureaucrats who do not know the "real" world of science. Many in administrative positions sometimes tend to think of scientists as fuzzy thinking, ivory-tower specialists who do not know the "real" world of politics.

How many times, on the other hand, have we thought in constructive terms about our relationship to each other? How many times have we thought that as scientists and as administrators we really need each other, in the ultimate sense of that word? In a job as manager of a large child and family development program known as Head Start, I have to effectively combine three ingredients—money and knowledge, plus good people at all administrative levels—to bring about a happy marriage between the first two. The key is knowledge. Without excellent scientific work, we obviously have an inadequate base from which to operate. The consequence is ineffective programs and, as a result, a waste of our tax dollars.

Our need is mutual. Scientists need the programs we have as market places for your products and the financial support that we can provide.

Managers and scientists must form a full blown partnership around one central theme: How can we as human beings better serve poor children? I am choosing the term "poor" deliberately because, while I recognize that there are middle-class families that have problems and needs, the needs of the poor are far more pervasive and debilitating. Since we are living in an era in which we must establish priorities because of inadequate resources, the needs of the poor are so overwhelming that they should be given maximum attention.

Scientists are well aware of the problem of getting their jobs done. I would like to relate some of the problems of administrators and describe how the scientist can help.

Consider the first basic problem. We in administrative positions at the Washington level must deal with many publics. Let me categorize two. First, there are those who control money. These include people from the Office of Economic Opportunity, the Budget Bureau, the White House staff, and, of course, the ultimate arbitrator, Congress. Within those groups who control how much Federal money is going to be made available for Head Start or other Federal child care programs, there are many who believe that child development and early childhood education should be a high priority item in the expenditure of Federal dollars. There is an equally vociferous group that believes this is a waste. They contend that the problems of poverty can best be solved by making people not poor through employment programs and income maintenance programs.

We have another public that we deal with, and it is a public that is becoming more vocal—the parents of Head Start children, the consumers. We never hear in discussions of the Westinghouse

Report[1] that 90% of the parents of Head Start thought the program was great. I challenge any public institution to come up with evidence of that kind of support for its program. The parents contend not only that it is great, but that they want more. Furthermore they are becoming more and more conscious of the fact that they have something to contribute to the development and administration of the program locally *and nationally*. We recently had a conference of local Head Start people in Washington. One of the products of that conference was a presentation of 19 resolutions to Secretary Finch by about 200 parents of Head Start children. They, in essence, said, "We not only want to be involved, we want to control this program at all levels." We see that one of our big jobs as administrators at the Federal level is to build some kind of bridge between the chasm of those who say "We want more, and we want to control it," and those who say, "It isn't worth it; Federal child care programming is not going to expand."

I can see only one way to get an answer to this question about whether the investment in early development and education is worthwhile. We need scientific evaluations of the effectiveness of various kinds of early childhood programs. We can say this is unfair, that no other social institution has to prove itself with this degree of precision. While this may be true, I do not believe it is all bad. Perhaps the absence of a demand for rigorous evaluation of some of the other institutions that have developed in our country over the past 100 years has resulted in a rigor mortis of those institutions. So I welcome that evaluation requirement. My hope is that those who are insisting upon it will recognize its extraordinary difficulties, that it will be many years before we obtain the quality answers we are looking for.

---

[1] The Westinghouse Report, a post hoc only assessment of the performance of Head Start and non-Head Start children in the first, second, and third grades of public school, found that there was little overall difference between the two groups. The Report has been widely cited as evidence that Head Start has "failed."

This is obviously not a picayune question. The answers, whenever they come, are going to be major determinants of public policy in this area. We cannot do a half-baked job of assessment. It must be done well. Public policy on this question is going to be decided largely by the kind of answers scientists provide and not in the kind of thinking that we, as nonscientists, engage in.

Now to a second major problem. Dr. Weikart, after reading what is being said about compensatory education, feels that the entire concept may be in deep trouble. He concludes that maybe it is more important to work with the very young, with infants. As Dr. Bruner says, not to remediate, but to begin the full process of development. I believe strongly that compensatory education at the elementary level, at the secondary level, and at the preschool level has not really been tested. While that jury is out, Head Start or some other organization like it, is going to continue. We as administrators have the here and now problem of deciding how to make it effective.

Right now we are getting conflicting answers. Dr. Weikart says "it ain't what you do, it's the way that you do it." There are equally distinguished scientists—Bettye Caldwell, Merl Karnes—who feel that the content of the curriculum *does* make a difference, some that group care is the answer, others that work should be done only with and through the family. Schaefer and Weikart and Kagan are of the opinion that parents (at least for the first two and a half years) are best in terms of providing input to young children. That is hardly surprising since middle-class parents have been performing the role reasonably successfully for generations.

Earl Schaefer says that environment plus socioeconomic status have an impact on intelligence. The question that we as administrators need an answer to is what specific ingredients in that environment have what kind of effect? What is the relationship of the development of intelligence to the school drop-out rate? Dr. Kagan feels that we must bring about basic changes in the ghetto and that ghetto residents must participate in decisions affecting them. Why not carry this one step further? Do we really mean ghetto involvement and parental involvement? What about ghetto control? What about parental control? Are we ready to face this? It is the logical next step. Or are we once again being paternalistic, as we so often have been? Another basic question is racism. What effect does it have on the problem?

What effect does all of this have on the things that we administrators are supposed to be doing? Essentially, we need good answers to these and many other questions about how children develop.

I would like to make some specific suggestions on how scientists can help us discover and disseminate information needed to develop more effective child development programming. First, researchers doing studies on the effects of intervention must follow their subjects into later years. We would be reluctant to fund any more "immediate impact only" intervention studies. The literature is now replete with studies which show that an immediate impact, using commonly accepted criteria, can be achieved. What we do not know is how long that impact lasts, under what conditions it will last. This we need to find out. It is a difficult and expensive problem to solve. A shorter study is neater, it is easier and yet it seems to us that we must focus even more on the long-range effects of what we do. This, after all, is the essence of development. Second, there must be continuity in the intervention process, whether it is begun in infancy or after. To get a true measure of effectiveness of a specific type of intervention, that same intervention technique should be continued through as many years as possible. This, too, is expensive and difficult, but a mandatory next step in our knowledge gathering processes.

Our need for more documentation of input is extraordinarily important. For the most part specific descriptions of what really went into the programs in many of the studies we have seen are sparse.

The basic question is: *What input, for what child, for how long, beginning and ending when, has what kind of effect?* To find the answers is an extraordinarily difficult task, yet if our knowledge is going to come to full fruition our efforts must be geared to this objective.

I would like to add one more thought. Earlier I suggested an alliance between scientists and administrators. I think there should be a third party involved. It will make life more difficult as most triangles do, and yet I think it is imperative. Unless we get the teacher training institutions and the education administration institutions involved, we are missing a vital line in the entire process. They, after all, are the principal agents of disseminating what the scientists discover. They must, therefore, become full partners, as early as possible.

In conclusion, I would like to stress several obvious points which, in our enthusiasm, we tend to overlook. First of all, in my judgment, the most compelling need that scientists in this field have is better instruments, instruments that are standardized for the entire population, not just white middle-class children. We must become considerably more sensitive to the influence of cultural differences on the standardization process.

Second, a common data base is badly needed. Project Upstart[2] is beginning to work on this. Third, it would be most helpful if, in publications, one indicated whether the findings were consistent or inconsistent with those commonly accepted in the field. To what extent does the author agree or disagree with others who have written on that subject? Such information would ease the process of assimilation and consolidation of the ever increasing amount of knowledge in this field.

Finally, the scientist must be aware that the kind of work he is involved with can very well be used as a basis for public policy.

[2] Project Upstart, an informal professional association, emerged from the concerns of infant development researchers that this field move in a coordinated way to resolve problems in implementation, evaluation and government/scientist relationships, and, by developing new approaches to sharing information and research activities, to accelerate the accumulation of knowledge in the field.

Witness the Westinghouse Report. Is he satisfied with the quality of work which he has published or plans to publish? Does he feel that his work could be used in part or as a whole as a basis for setting public policy? Whether the scientist realizes it or not, his published work carries with it that possibility.

I hope I have conveyed that I am for scientific research, *good* research. Excellent work has been done in this field, as has sloppy work, just as there have been good administrators of public programs and ineffective ones. Moreover, until a competent jury convicts compensatory early childhood education of being irrelevant, I favor it 100%. Bettye Caldwell (1969)[3] –expresses well my concluding thoughts.

> In our enthusiasm for early education it is easy to promise too much. When too much is promised, a little disappointment seems like a lot. Or to use an expression I have used on other occasions, "The natural sequel to oversell is overkill." It is my fervent hope that in our current enthusiasm for early intervention we do not try to oversell ourselves to the point where we cannot deliver and thus be forced into another early demise. We do not need another renaissance of interest in early childhood. We only need to make certain that the current interest fulfills its obligation [p.10].

REFERENCES

Caldwell, B. M. The rationale for early intervention. Paper presented at the Early Childhood Education Conference of the Council for Exceptional Children, New Orleans, December, 1969.

[3]*Editor's note.* Dr. Caldwell had been invited to participate in this symposium, but was unable to attend.

Chapter 9

Some Considerations Concerning Day-Care Centers | *Victor H. Denenberg*

I should like to comment briefly on the papers of the various participants emphasizing those points which I think are relevant to the question of immediate concern, *viz.*, what considerations should be involved in setting up day-care centers for infants? Kagan notes that 12 years of formal education is now a necessity for economic survival in our highly technical society, and that children from poor families have a high rate of school failures. Although recognizing that genetic factors probably contribute in part to the incidence of school failure, he presents a strong argument that the vast majority of failures by children from deprived environments are primarily a function of experience. One of Kagan's suggestions for reducing school failure among poor children is to change the nature of the caretaker-infant relationship on the assumption that a child's experiences with his adult caretaker during the first 24 months of life are major determinants of the quality of his motivation, expectancy of success, and cognitive abilities during his school years. He suggests that the poor mother has feelings of exploitation by society and a sense of futility with respect to her capability to influence society and, more important, to influence the growth and development of her own child. He states that "If we could increase the

125

mother's sense of control over her infant's growth and persuade her of the value of language, motivation, and expectancy of success, she might begin to believe that her efforts with the infant could facilitate fulfillment of her ideals."

Kagan lists seven major sets of differences which he believes exist between poor children and middle-class children. These are: language, mental set, attachment, inhibition, a sense of effectiveness, motivation, and expectancy of failure. Some support for these theoretical notions comes from his longitudinal and his cross-sectional development studies. Especially important to note here is his experimental findings that middle-class mothers spent much more time vocalizing with their babies than did lower-class mothers. This is empirical confirmation of Kagan's ideas concerning differences in language behavior between these two groups.

Mason's paper is concerned with the development of intelligence within a comparative biological framework, with particular attention to the effects of early deprivation upon intellectual development. As he points out, the human infant is a biological organism and in order to fully understand how it comes to be a mature civilized human being an understanding of its biological and evolutionary history is needed. Much of our fundamental understanding concerning the processes involved in early growth and development have come about through experimental studies with animals, and Mason indicates that this is probably true for our understanding of intelligence as well. With respect to intelligence, he develops the very useful concept that there is more openness in the schemas of animals as one ascends the phyletic scale, ultimately culminating in man. The advantages of having a more open system includes greater sensory differentiation, increased differentiation of motor acts, and increased integrative capacities. Man is uniquely outstanding on the last of these three items. In general, the advantages of an open system is that the individual has greater flexibility in his behavior. The critical disadvantage of an open system according to Mason is "...that initial schemas are often functionally unstable, if not incomplete. Open schemas presumably require input as a source of stability and a means of filling 'gaps.' If this is true, we would anticipate that the 'open' organism deprived of certain critical experiences early in life will be seriously handicapped in its later adjustments." His review of the literature indicates that there are at least six consequences of early deprivation upon an open system. In ascending order these are: breakdown of the primordial schemas; lack of environmental "tuning"; distortion of schemas; excessive arousal effects, deficiencies in problem-solving skills; and curtailment of higher-order functions. Analogs of each of these six characteristics may be found in human beings reared under deprivational conditions.

Mason's summary of learning sets data is particularly relevant here. A learning set is a generalized concept developed by an animal as a function of lengthy exposure to a variety of problems within a particular class. Evidence has been found that this skill is roughly ordered along a phylogenetic continuum. Learning sets is certainly the closest thing we have to a measure of "intelligence" on a comparative basis. Of direct interest to us is the finding that chimpanzees—one of the highest nonhuman primates and, therefore, an animal with a very "open" system—who had been raised in isolation for the first 2 years of life and who had then spent 5 years in complex and enriched environments in a group living situation, were still markedly deficient in discrimination learning-set formation as compared to a control group who had lived in the jungle for the first 2 years of life. Thus, we see with this near ancestor of man that 5 years of normal living experiences could not overcome the intellectual deficits produced by the lack of stimulation during the first 2 years of life.

In this regard it is important to emphasize Mason's conclusion that openness does not create intelligence, but that it establishes conditions under which the growth of intelligence is possible. Thus, the experiences which the organism receives are extremely critical with respect to whether the open system is able to grow and develop in the normal fashion or not. In fact, given an open system it is mandatory that we be especially careful concerning the quantity and quality of experiences which the organism receives. In this framework Kagan's findings that lower-class mothers do not vocalize as much to their babies as middle-class mothers may well be an example of the ill consequences of failing to input the appropriate types of information to a very open system.

Papoušek's chapter contains a wealth of useful information and advice concerning the advantages and dangers in raising infants in a day-care center. Some of the advantages are: raising the level of educational care; positively influencing the development of social behavior and speech; facilitating the transfer of important educational principles to the families involved; and setting up other proper conditions for the infant's development, such as adequate nutrition, space for play, and preventative medical measures.

He also provides us with a list of risks which may result from the institutional nature of day-care centers, including: impersonal care and poor emotional contact between children and adults; a neglect of individual differences because of a normative approach which tends to stress conformity; absence of males, over-excitement brought about by social interaction which can result in stress; potential increase in epidemiological risk because of homogeneity of age; a decrease in parents' feelings of responsibility because of the care provided by the day center with consequent maternal or paternal deprivation; and the possibility of a slowdown in the development of speech and cognition because the child is kept away from the broader environment involved in adult human activities and complex speech patterns.

Papoušek rightly stresses the concern with the quality of stimulation involved in day-care center experiences. He also stresses that day-care centers cannot substitute successfully for parents and recommends that the parents should be encouraged to keep the children in the center for the minimum time necessary. He raises the very important practical and theoretical issue as to the effects of placing children into centers at 6 months of age. He points out, and several research studies support him, that separation of the infant from the family before 6 months of age is much easier for the infant with respect to his ability to adapt than is separation after 6 months of age. If the infant has difficulty in adjusting to a day-care center, Papoušek advises that the infant only spend a short time in the center with his mother for the first several days or weeks until the child becomes adapted to the new environment.

It is also important to note some of the bad effects of day-care center experience which Papoušek discusses. Children raised in these conditions show delay in the development of speech, oculomotor coordination, and social behavior. Knowing this, it is possible to build in experiences which will prevent these deficits from occurring. Finally, one must be continually aware of the possibility of increased morbidity from raising infants or children in day-care centers. The actual cause of increased morbidity is not known, but physiological and psychogenic factors are probably intimately involved. Here, too, a proper regimen and an alert staff would be able to prevent this.

In his paper Schaefer develops the thesis that formal educational experiences should begin at birth and continue through maturity. The need for very early education may be shown as follows. Typically, early school experience does not increase the low levels of intellectual functioning that disadvantaged children have at the time of entrance into school. Paralleling this is the finding that mean differences between various social groups in intelligence test performance may be established prior to 3 years of age. In addition, there is a relatively high correlation between intelligence test performance at 3 years and in early adulthood. On the other hand, one usually does not find a consistent relationship between intelligence test scores and socioeconomic status prior to 15 months of life.

Schaefer proposes that early educational experience must start before the onset of language development (which is the most important component of the IQ test) in order to prevent the low levels of intellectual functioning that will develop prior to school entrance as well as to increase the rate of intellectual development during the school years.

In addition to this specific hypothesis, which he supports by empirical evidence, Schaefer proposes a more general hypothesis to the effect that an increase in stimulation will bring about an increase in mental test scores while termination of educational intervention will result in a decrease in test scores. In his review he covers a number of studies which support this hypothesis and rather clearly indicate that any "one-shot" intervention program will not have a long-lasting effect upon the intellectual capabilities of the child.

One of the things that Schaefer emphasized, as did others, is that the stability of IQ scores may be an artifact brought about by raising children in relatively stable environments. By significantly changing the nature of the environment, it seems now rather evident that one can significantly increase IQ scores. A consequence of this conclusion is to lay to rest an erroneous interpretation from Bloom's study on intellectual development. Bloom concluded from certain statistical data that approximately 50% of the intelligence of the average 17-year-old is present by age 4. This carries with it both a strong genetic connotation as well as a strong implication of irreversibility. Of course, neither of these conclusions follows logically from the data, especially when one realizes that the children in Bloom's study were reared in relatively stable environments. As Schaefer points out, if children of 4 years of age were randomly assigned to different environments, there would probably be less predictability with respect to later intelligence test performance.

In this general context another one of Schaefer's conclusions is worth noting: namely, that different environments may have different potentials for maintaining or fostering intellectual functioning. Thus, one of the objectives of any research program would be to find those environments which tend to maximize the individual's potential for intellectual activities. Coupled with this should be the realization that there are many different factors in the environment which can bring about lowered intellectual performance (e.g., malnutrition, maternal neglect, lack of verbal stimulation, and impoverished environment) so that the kind of experimental regimen which might maximize or facilitate intellectual development for one class of deficiencies may not have any effect on a child reared under a different set of environmental deficits.

Finally, Schaefer reviews a set of studies indicating the importance of the mother's behavior with respect to the intellectual development of the child and concludes by commenting on two successful preschool educational programs—one by Weikart, the other by Gray and Klaus—which included the training of the parents as an integral part of the program.

Like Schaefer, Weikart and Lambie agree that education should start in infancy. Their argument is that infant education offers the greatest "room for action" to improve the intellectual growth of the child. A major conclusion drawn by Weikart and Lambie from their comparative research on preschool curricula—indeed, a conclusion which has vast implications for the whole question of infant and preschool education if its generality can be broadly established—is that the specific nature of the curriculum is not important as far as the infant's or child's intellectual growth and development is concerned. What is important is that the curriculum, whichever one it may be, be structured and have a wide range of experiences to offer the youngster. Weikart and Lambie point out that the major function of the curriculum is to structure or guide the teacher's activities and to challenge the teacher. They also state that the success of the program is dependent, not upon the particular curriculum, but upon the intimate involvement of the teachers and staff members. This conclusion has a drastic effect upon the underlying assumptions and philosophy of a preschool education program because it shifts the focus of attention away from planning *the* curriculum and, as Weikart and Lambie say, ". . .permits clear program focus on the mother as a primary teacher of her own child with specific curriculum being her own invention. The role of the teacher is to assist and supervise the mother in this process."

The approach used by Weikart and Lambie is to have the teacher go to the home of the mother and infant, where the teacher assumes a "low power" status with all attention focused upon the interest of the infant. The teacher visits the house once each week and spends approximately an hour there. Thus, a teacher could visit a number of houses in a week's time. The Weikart and Lambie program, therefore, may be considered to be complementary to a day-care center program and to be very useful in those many instances where it is not possible for a mother to utilize day-care facilities because of the necessity that she remain at home.

The Weikart and Lambie description of the interaction of a teacher with a mother and child at home emphasizes the lack of information that we have concerning the behavior patterns and attitudes of underprivileged families with respect to infants. An intensive descriptive analysis, with an ethological as well as psychological orientation, of family interactions in underprivileged homes would be of considerable value and may be a necessary precondition for any completely successful educational or intervention program.

Among the many cogent points which the two discussants made, a few should be emphasized. Bruner wishes to change the orientation of early assistance programs from a "therapeutic" philosophy to one aimed at maximizing the fullness of one's growth. He suggests that we consider abandoning such terms as "intervention" and "remedy," both of which have the implication of trying to improve an already bad situation. Instead, the orientation should be that of aiding the young to grow in order to "...achieve their fullness as men and women..." He suggests that we should be concerned with "...the provision of the kind of environment necessary for growth, whatever one's parents' skin color, religion, pocketbook, origin, or genetic structure." Bruner points out that a "one-shot" intervention program will not achieve this aim, and he argues convincingly that when we originate early assistance programs we assume a responsibility for these young people throughout their life cycle, not merely during their preschool days, nursery school hours, or street life.

Although primarily practical matters have been discussed this cannot be divorced from underlying theory, and Bruner has made two sharp comments that merit considerable thought. First, we must view development within a much broader framework and consider how best to integrate our ideas of education within such a framework. Much education takes place outside of the classroom and, as Schaefer strongly emphasized in his paper, major portions of one's educational experience occur before the child ever enters any formal classroom situation. Bruner has put this nicely with his statement that "We plainly need a theory of education whose pedagogy is not school bound." At the level of psychological theory he points out that most contemporary theories of intellectual or cognitive development do not consider the reciprocal relationship between the caretaker and an infant, and yet it is apparent from all of the papers as well as the findings of a great many other research studies that this dyadic interaction between caretaker and infant is of critical importance for the physical, psychological, and social growth of the child.

Bruner raised important philosophical and theoretical issues. Orton has raised equally important methodological and measurement questions which we have to face. He asks: "What inputs, for what child, for how long, beginning and ending when, has what kind of effect?" The answer to this question requires that we specify the population of infants and children that are sampled, the specific experiences to which these children are exposed by the researchers including the length of time of the exposure and the patterning of the various experiences, and the long-term consequences of these experiences. Orton points out that this kind of information is necessary in order for rational policy decisions to be made. He emphasizes the need for better measurement instruments which are standardized on wider populations than merely white middle-class children. This tough-minded empirical attitude is familiar to one who has spent his professional life amidst experimental psychologists and psychometricians, and it is encouraging and gratifying that such an attitude is present at a key policy decision-making level.

In conclusion, it is apparent that we have many rich and

varied ideas as to what should be done in an infant day-care center. Certain common ideas run through all of the comments and include such points as the necessity of getting the mother actively involved with her child, enriching the environment of the child, and, possibly most important, arranging the conditions so that the infant will interact instrumentally with his environment and will receive positive feedback from the environment as a function of that interaction. Everyone is also in agreement that the educational process should begin at birth or as soon thereafter as is feasible, and that the caretaker, whether it be a mother or some other figure, has a tremendously important role to play in the education and training of the infant.

However, even with these generalities, the fundamental question remains: How do we put all of this together into a regimen of experiences to maximize the physical, psychological, and social growth potential of the infant? This is the question of the curriculum, and Weikart's finding suggests that this may be less important than we had previously thought. In order to answer the question raised above and to determine the generality of Weikart's conclusion, it is necessary to have a large scale experimental investigation coupled with long-term assessment using good psychometric instruments. Such a program can only be done with federal funding. I suggest the necessity of setting up at least two federally funded experimental day-care centers in large urban areas in different parts of the country in order to answer the questions raised here. Within each center a number of different experimental regimens (or curricula) would be set up and tried out, with appropriate control groups. The assessment must go beyond the usual paper-and-pencil or developmental norms approach, and should recognize that the child lives in his own naturalistic environment. Thus, a proper assessment should utilize the philosophical approach and the techniques of the ethologists who have continually stressed the necessity of studying the behavior patterns of the organism in its natural setting as well as psychological measurement.

We should not concentrate upon those measures which are easiest to obtain or which appear to be most reliable (e.g., developmental schedules, verbal skills), but should recognize that in the natural world of man social interactions and that amorphous thing which we call "personality" are, in the ultimate sense, most important. The fact that our measuring instruments for these kinds of variables are poor is no reason for ignoring them. Indeed, this is all the more reason for us to be concerned about assessing these dimensions of behavior.

The above suggestions merely outline what I believe to be an absolutely necessary program of research and development if we wish to understand how the infant grows, adapts, and learns to live in the world into which he is born. It is very obvious that such a program will be quite expensive. However, industry and the military learned a long time ago the great value of investing money in research and development, and they literally spend millions of dollars each year to assess and evaluate their products. The most important product we have in this country are our children. Can we afford to do less to assess the effectiveness of their educational experiences when we realize that these experiences initiate the whole chain of reactions which culminate in a mature man or woman?

Subject Index